Blades & Owls

A pictorial history of the Sheffield derby matches

THIS BOOK HAS
BEEN PUBLISHED
IN A LIMITED
EDITION OF WHICH
THIS IS

Number   331

A LIST OF THE
ORIGINAL SUBSCRIBERS TO THE
LIMITED EDITION MAY BE
FOUND AT THE BACK
OF THE BOOK

Blades & Owls

A pictorial history of the Sheffield derby matches

The Star

Keith Farnsworth

Breedon Books
Publishing Company
Derby

First published in Great Britain by
The Breedon Books Publishing Company Limited
44 Friar Gate, Derby, DE1 1DA.
1995

ISBN 1 85983 036 6

Printed and bound by Butler & Tanner, Frome, Somerset.
Cover printed by Premier Print, Nottingham.

Contents

Acknowledgements

We are grateful to the following who have loaned photographs and illustrations which have proved so invaluable in supplementing those drawn from the files of *The Star:* Howard Johnson, Keith Bannister, Stan Hathaway, George McCabe, and our good friend Roger Oldfield at Northends.

Especial thanks to Keith Howard for the loan of programmes from his extensive collection; and to John Brodie and Jason Dickinson, two great enthusiasts whose passion for research and records helped provide important additional background – Jason's contribution including helping dig out some of those long-lost Harry Heap cartoons which were once such a familiar part of the local sporting scene and a regular feature in *The Star* and *Green 'Un.*

It has also been helpful to talk to many old players and former colleagues, including Graham Shaw, Joe Shaw, Don Megson, Alf Ringstead, Vin 'Mick' Kenny, Benny Hill, Peter Harvey and Stuart Machin; and, in terms of local football writers whose reports have helped in the compilation of the story of Sheffield derby days, it does seem appropriate here to pay tribute to men like Richard A.Sparling, Dudley Blake, Keith Gardiner, Fred Walters, 'Taffy' Williams, Monty Marston, Peter Cooper, John Hathaway, Ross Jenkinson, Peter Howard, Tony Hardisty, Dave Pardon, Peter Markie. They have left their mark on Sheffield football with their reports. Of course, the modern inheritors of a great local journalistic tradition are Tony Pritchett (who has the distinction of being 'transferred' from Wednesday to United during his long service with *The Star*) and Paul Thompson.

We owe much to the photographers whose pictures are featured here, and especial thanks to Steve Ellis; also Brenda, Nicola, Bette and Jacqui in the Sheffield Newspapers library, and assistant editor Peter Goodman.

A final thanks to Anton Rippon at Breedon Books, and, once again, the author's wife, Linda, for invaluable help in proof reading.

Introduction

This book celebrates more than 100 years of Sheffield derby matches and the great rivalry between Wednesday and United over a series spanning some 240 games since the first meeting at Olive Grove in December 1890.

It also serves as a dual tribute: to the famous and oft-forgotten Blades and Owls favourites whose names will endure in the history of this special fixture, and to generations of supporters for whom derby day has invariably held pride of place on the local football calendar. Enjoy your trip down Memory Lane!

FOR THE RECORD 1890-1995

		Blades		**Owls**	**Blades**	**Owls**
	P	wins	draws	wins	goals	goals
League	98	37	30	31	139	128
FA Cup	9	3	3	3	14	13
League Cup	2	0	1	1	1	3
Zenith Data	1	0	0	1	2	3
	110	40	34	36	156	147

The Sheffield teams have also met 129 times in club, friendly, testimonial, County Cup and other senior fixtures, with United boasting 49 wins to Wednesday's 48 in these games.

Thus the overall record presently stands at 239 matches, 89 United wins and 84 Wednesday wins, with 66 draws as at the end of the 1994-95 season.

Heap cartoon of Ozzie Owl and Bertie Blade, reading the Green 'Un with the famous Alf looking on.

The First Sheffield Derbies

Monday, 15 December 1890: Wednesday 2 United 1

Monday, 12 January 1891: United 3 Wednesday 2

IT WAS in 1890 that Sheffield football fans had their first experience of derby day drama when the heroes of Wednesday and United finally came face to face at Olive Grove on a raw December afternoon shrouded in the fog and smoke symbolic of the steel and cutlery town in that late Victorian age.

The game was played against a background of mutual ill-feeling between officials of the clubs, with Wednesday, founded in 1867 but a professional outfit for barely three years, still upset about the decision of the Bramall

Lane committee to form a rival club in the spring of 1889.

No fixture in the history of the game in the town had generated so much enthusiasm among supporters and a crowd of around 10,000 made the journey up Queen's Road (not far from United's headquarters) and over the railway bridge into the compact little ground that had been Wednesday's home since they reluctantly adopted professionalism in 1887.

At another time, Wednesday would have gone into this historic duel full of confidence, but, ironically, the club that had been FA Cup Finalists and first champions of the Football Alliance the previous season were enduring a lean spell and stood bottom of the table after only one win in ten games. And, as United were thriving in the Midland League, where they would finish fifth, it was no surprise that the bookmakers parading round the ground rated them firm favourites.

Wednesday's team included two England players. One you couldn't miss, for Teddy Brayshaw was so proud of his solitary international cap that he always insisted on wearing it in matches! The other was battling centre-half Billy Betts, whose full-time job was in the Neepsend Gas Works. The home side also boasted a new signing, Harry Brandon, who followed his cousin Bob Brandon from Clyde. United had two men, backs Harry Lilley and Mick Whitham, who would become the club's first capped stars within two years, while Rab Howell would represent his country by 1895.

United, kicking towards the

The first Sheffield derby in the Football League was played at Bramall Lane in October 1893 and ended in a 1-1 draw, Hill scoring for United and Spiksley for Wednesday. The teams in this Division One fixture were:

United: Howlett; Whitham, Cain, Howell, Hendry, Needham, Gallacher, Fleming, Hill, Hammond, Drummond.

Wednesday: Allan; Earp, Langley, Brandon, Betts, Jamieson, Webster, Davis, J. Miller, Brady, Spiksley.

When the return fixture was staged at Bramall Lane in November, United won 2-1 with goals from Drummond and Hammond, Miller replying for Wednesday.

The first time Wednesday beat United in a League game was in September 1895 when a goal from Lawrence Bell earned the points at Owlerton.

Town End in the first half, confirmed themselves as the form team in those opening 45 minutes, and led at the interval

thanks to a 20th-minute goal from 'Dundee' Robertson. But

Olive Grove, scene of the first Sheffield derby in December 1890.

A Wednesday team of 1890. Back row (left to right): Jack Dungworth, Teddy Brayshaw, John Holmes (president), Jim Smith, W.Fearnehough (vice-president), H.A.Morley, A.C. 'Clinks' Mumford, Henry Pearson (secretary). Middle row: H.Woolhouse, Billy Betts, George Waller, Tom Cawley, Arthur Nixon (treasurer). Front row: Harry Winterbottom, Billy Ingram, 'Micky' Bennett. Note: Waller later joined United and became one of the Bramall Lane club's most faithful servants as an outstanding trainer right up to the early 1930s. Bennett's brother, Walter, later had a great career with Sheffield United.

Wednesday displayed a dramatic improvement in the second period and, after 'Toddles' Woolhouse had headed them level, little Harry Winterbottom marked his benefit year with his most important goal of the season – the 85th-minute winner which Charlie Howlett, the Grenoside-based goalkeeper famed for insisting on playing in spectacles, admitted he never saw!

The return fixture was staged at Bramall Lane exactly four weeks later, and was the first of many occasions in Sheffield derby history when United recovered from a two-goal deficit to win – to the delight of their followers in the 14,000 crowd.

The only change in the teams was the appearance of Billy Ingram for the injured Betts in Wednesday's line-up,

> In those days Wednesday were known as the 'Blades', while United's nickname was the 'Cutlers', though, for a time, they were often called the 'Junior Blades'.

and he was the man who broke the deadlock with the game's first goal 20 minutes into the

J.C.Clegg, the referee in the first Sheffield derby and a soccer leader linked with both clubs.

Ernest Needham, a great United hero who arrived on the scene in 1891.

The 1890 Line-up:

Wednesday	**United**
Jim Smith	Charlie Howlett
Fred Thompson	Harry Lilley
Teddy Brayshaw	Mick Whitham
Harry Brandon	E.Cross
Billy Betts*	Rab Howell
Tom Cawley	George Groves
Harry Winterbottom	W.Calder
Arthur Mumford	Arthur Watson
Bob Brandon	W.Robertson
Harry Woolhouse	W.L.Bridgewater
W.Hodder	Bernard L.Shaw

*replaced by Billy Ingram in second game.
Referee: J.C.Clegg

second half. Within three minutes, Bob Brandon increased Wednesday's lead, and United looked set for another defeat. However, Ecclesfielder Arthur Watson quickly reduced arrears. Then Rab Howell, a future England player remembered for having been born in a gypsy caravan at Wincobank, equalised with a speculative long shot which deceived Jim Smith (his real name was Clarke) in the Wednesday goal; and, with five minutes remaining, Calder grabbed the winner as the men from Olive Grove protested bitterly that the United forward had been 'miles off-side'.

The Bitter FA Cup Marathon of 1900

THE intense rivalry between Wednesday and United in the Victorian era was never better illustrated than in the bitter FA Cup battles of February 1900 – a month of heavy snow and freezing weather which was in sharp contrast to the heated emotions this 'marathon' duel generated on the Sheffield football scene.

When the second-round draw paired the Steel City clubs in the national knock-out competition for the first time, fans of that era witnessed a furious feud fought over three eventful meetings in ten days.

United were the Cup holders and led Division One, while Wednesday were second in Division Two and pushing for instant promotion in their first-ever season in the lower grade; but the success both clubs were enjoying was not reflected in the quality of the play.

The first match, watched by 32,381 at Bramall Lane, was abandoned at 0-0 by referee John Lewis after 50 minutes owing to a snowstorm. Further snow prompted a postponement in midweek, and it was only after volunteers had cleared the pitch that the tie went ahead on the following Saturday when a 28,374 crowd turned up.

This was the game in which tempers flared and the spectacle suddenly turned ugly in an over-physical second half in which Wednesday suffered a triple blow. Goalkeeper Jimmy Massey took a severe knock, the legendary winger Fred Spiksley was carried off with a damaged knee, and Harry Millar finished up a passenger. Fouls became too numerous to record, noted a reporter, who said the only positive facts were the Archie Brash goal which had given Wednesday the lead after 20 minutes, and Jack Almond's 80th-minute equaliser for United.

When the replay was staged at Wednesday's new Owlerton ground two days later, the

Ambrose Langley, a famous Wednesday captain who played in 20 Sheffield derby games in League and FA Cup. He was one of two men sent off in the final game of the 1900 'marathon' and conceded the penalty from which Needham gave United the lead.

John Pryce, the Scot, who played for Hibernian before arriving in Sheffield via Glossop, was sent off in the 1900 Cup battle at Owlerton.

Harry Millar, another of Wednesday's Scottish signings, arrived at Owlerton via Bury and Reading, and, at 5ft 7in tall, he made a big impact in the successful push for promotion, but suffered an injury in the first FA Cup clash and missed the replay.

James Massey, the goalkeeper who was one of three Wednesday injury victims in the Bramall Lane clash of 1900. The man from the Black Country joined the Owls from Doncaster Rovers. He missed the replay, with Mallinson standing in.

Press called for both teams to 'bury the hatchet', but the mood in the home camp was not improved when Massey, Millar and Spiksley all reported unfit. Mallinson, Lee and Topham deputised. Meanwhile, United were at full strength.

The clash of Monday, 19 February 1900, which attracted a 23,000 crowd, has passed into local sporting folklore as

The Owlerton Cup Battle Line-up;	
Wednesday	**United**
Mallinson	Foulke
Layton	Thickett
Langley	Boyle
Ferrier	Johnson
Crawshaw	Morren
Ruddlesdin	Needham
Brash	Bennett
Pryce	Beer
Lee	Hedley
Wright	Almond
Topham	Priest

the fiercest derby of them all, described as 'a disgrace... a game of wild excitement which badly tarnished the image of Sheffield football'.

Wednesday finished with eight men, after two players, John Pryce and skipper Ambrose Langley, were sent off, and a third home hero, George Lee, was carried off with a broken leg.

United ended up with nine after losing forwards George Hedley and Walter Bennett

Fred Priest was a great favourite at Bramall Lane and a maker as well as a taker of goals.

Fred Spiksley played in 17 League and Cup derbies for Wednesday but missed the Owlerton replay of 1900 after being carried off with a damaged knee in the Bramall Lane clash.

Sheffield United, League Champions in 1897-98. Back row (players only): Hedley, Johnson, Boyle, Foulke, Almond, Morren. Front row: Bennett, Beer, Needham, Thickett, Priest.

with serious injuries. The Blades won 2-0, but it detracted from the merit of their victory that when Ernest Needham put them ahead from the penalty-spot just after half-time Wednesday were down to ten men; and, by the time Billy Beer settled the issue with a late goal, there were only 17 players on the pitch (most of them limping) and the match had turned into a shambles.

Contemporary match report.

Derby Day Goal Kings

The names of Harry Johnson, Jimmy Dunne and Bill Boyd have a special place in Bramall Lane's Hall of Fame because these United heroes all scored three or more goals in derby duels with Wednesday in the inter-war years.

HARRY JOHNSON, the Ecclesfield product who holds United's all-time aggregate record with 225 goals between 1919 and 1931, became the first man in local football history to grab a hat-trick in a major Sheffield derby, on the afternoon of 22 February 1928

when he struck three times in the space of 18 second-half minutes to help the Blades to a 4-1 victory in an FA Cup fifth-round replay at Bramall Lane.

Ironically, Johnson was limited to only two goals in Football League derbies with the Owls, although he did

Harry Johnson (centre) reminisces about the art of goalscoring with two heroes of the 1970s, Billy Dearden (left) and United's post-war record marksman Alan Woodward.

15

manage five other goals, including four which helped United win the County Cup on three separate occasions between 1921 and 1926. Johnson's father, 'Old' Harry (in the Victorian era) and his younger brother, Tom (a Blades captain in the 1930s) also figured in United teams in derby duels with Wednesday.

Irish international **JIMMY DUNNE** had the distinction of scoring 17 goals (including four doubles) in matches against the Owls, but his most famous feat was performed at Bramall Lane on Monday, 10 October 1932 when he found the net four times in the Blades' 4-2 win in what was described as one of the best in the long series of County Cup Finals.

Dunne had a reputation as one of the finest headers of the ball ever seen in Sheffield, and, not surprisingly perhaps, three of his goals on this occasion were scored with his head – with the fourth being a tap-in from a rebound after he had headed against the bar!

Two of his goals came in the first-half, after three and 33 minutes, and his others both came in the space of two minutes midway through the second half with the Owls having twice hauled themselves level with strikes from Harry Burgess and Ronnie Starling.

United: Kendall; J.R.Gibson, Green, Gooney, Holmes, Hall, Oxley, Barclay, Dunne, Pickering, Oswald.

Wednesday: Breedon; Walker, Blenkinsop, Strange, Leach, Malloch, Hooper, Starling, Ball, Burgess, Rimmer.

When United sold Dunne to Arsenal in 1933, his

Jimmy Dunne

replacement was a Scot called **BILL BOYD,** and he marked his derby debut at Bramall Lane on 3 March 1934 with the only First Division hat-trick notched in a match between the Sheffield clubs.

This was one of those days when the Blades came from behind to triumph, and they did so in style by turning a 1-0 half-time deficit – Horace Burrows had scored for Wednesday after only three

minutes – into a 5-1 victory. It was a badly needed success, for United were battling against relegation and, sadly, it was a struggle in which they failed and so lost their top-grade status after 41 years.

Boyd – his tussle with Walter Millership was a great feature of the match – launched the home recovery after 65 minutes when heading in an Alec Stacey cross after beating goalkeeper Jack Brown to the ball. Then, after Jack Pickering had shot the Blades in front in the 75th minute, Boyd completed his hat-trick with strikes after 79 and 88 minutes. Stacey headed United's fifth a minute from the end.

United: Kendall; Anderson, Wilkinson, Stacey, Holmes, Gooney, Williams, Barclay, Boyd, Pickering, Oswald.

Wednesday: Brown; Walker, Catlin, Leach, Millership, Burrows, Hooper, Starling, Dewar, Burgess, Rimmer.

It is sometimes forgotten that two Wednesday men scored notable hat-tricks in matches which are seldom accorded 'major' status.

DOUGLAS HUNT once scored three goals for Wednesday in a 4-1 defeat of United in a match arranged at Hillsborough on 20 August 1938 to mark the Football League's Golden Jubilee.

Douglas Hunt

JACKIE ROBINSON twice repeated the feat in wartime games. He scored three in a 3-3 draw at Bramall Lane in November 1941, and claimed another treble in the famous derby at Hillsborough on 13 February 1943 when the Owls romped to an 8-2 triumph in which Frank Melling (later to

Jackie Robinson

become a Blades director) scored twice and Jack Thompson also claimed a double. Reynolds got the other, and, for the record, Albert Nightingale and Jack Pickering got United's consolation goals.

It should also be noted that **CHARLIE THOMPSON** scored three for United in a 3-1 defeat of Wednesday at Bramall Lane on 6 February 1943, ten days before the Owls enjoyed that memorable revenge.

Derby Day Goal Heroes

CHARLIE TOMLINSON scored a remarkable goal for Wednesday against United in a Football League North wartime match at Bramall Lane on 8 September 1945. Wednesday were attacking the Shoreham Street 'Kop' end in

the second half when Tomlinson (always known as 'Shadows') tried to lift a bouncing ball over the head of Blades' full-back Fred Furniss. He succeeded only in sending it straight up into the air, but then elected to head it over both Furniss and Alf Toothill in turn, and, finally, he volleyed the dipping ball past goalkeeper Jack Smith. Wednesday won 3-1 with their other goals coming from Jackie Robinson and Jack Lindsay. United's consolation strike came from Bert Knott. Tomlinson scored four wartime goals against United, all in 1945.

TEDDY GLENNON, a bustling Wednesday centre-forward who served the club from 1910 to 1919, made a big impact on the derby scene during the years of World War One, claiming ten goals for the Owls in this period – including four in a 5-0 victory at Bramall Lane in March 1916. However, the Denaby product, who had notched four goals in pre-war League derbies, had failed to score in the Lane clash with the Blades in the previous January. In fact, he and United's Bill Brelsford were sent off for fighting after 25 minutes in this game. The Blades man was alleged to have elbowed Glennon in a goalmouth incident which provoked fighting between rival players, and United skipper George Utley emerged with a bloody nose. The upshot was that both teams finished the first half with only nine men on the field – Wednesday's Frank Womack and United's Oliver Tummon having both gone off injured after Tummon had given the Blades the lead. Capper salvaged a draw for the Owls with a goal ten minutes from the end.

Bill Punton

Bill Punton, an emergency buy from Norwich City in November 1966, managed only 16 League outings for United and scored only

one goal, but it earned him a place in derby day folklore. It just happened to be the winner in the 1-0 defeat of Wednesday in a First Division duel at Bramall Lane on 4 February 1967.

Derek Pace, a £12,000 signing from Aston Villa who played for United from 1957 to 1964 and claimed a post-war scoring record with 163 goals in 294 League and Cup matches, scored six times in League derbies with Wednesday and also notched five in County Cup games with the Owls. His first goal in a League derby came in a 1-0 victory at Bramall Lane in February 1959 when a 43,919 crowd saw him nip in for a typical opportunist strike when Peter Swan let a bouncing ball run through to Ron Springett. Pace also notched a double in a 2-1 success at Hillsborough in February 1962.

Andrew Wilson, Wednesday's most prolific marksman, scored 11 goals in League derbies with the Blades. His first came in 1-0 victories for the Owls in April and November 1901. His last derby goal was in a 1-1 draw at Hillsborough in 1915

Johnny Fantham set a new post-

Derek Pace

Johnny Fantham

Alan Birchenall

David Layne

war League aggregate scoring record for Wednesday when he scored in the 1-1 draw with United at Hillsborough in January 1968. It was his 141st League goal and took him past Redfern Froggatt's tally. Lanky Mick Hill scored for United in this game, and it was set up by little Willie Carlin, who celebrated by running to the spectators standing in front of the south stand and kissing the first woman he spotted in the red-and-white scarf!

Alan Birchenall was just a teenager with a solitary League appearance to his name, made three days earlier, when he made his Sheffield derby debut for the Blades before a 32,684 crowd at Hillsborough on 5 September 1964 and scored both goals in a 2-0 defeat of Wednesday in a First Division fixture. Birchenall, nicknamed 'Sherman', hit the target six times in his first four outings against the Owls. He grabbed another double in a 2-2 draw at Wednesday's ground in March 1966 and scored the winner in a 1-0 success at Bramall Lane in September 1965. The blond striker was on the losing side only twice in his seven League derby outings against the Owls.

David Layne scored five goals in four League derbies, including doubles at Bramall Lane in a 2-2 draw in October 1962 and in the Hillsborough return in May 1963 when the Owls won 3-1.

Jimmy Trotter twice scored two goals against United but finished on the losing side — in 1925 and 1926.

John Ritchie scored the only goal of the game to give Wednesday the points in the derby at Bramall Lane in September 1967.

Jimmy Trotter

John Ritchie

BOBBY DAVISON, who scored two goals for United on his Sheffield derby debut in the famous 3-1 win at Hillsborough in March 1992, also scored the 90th minute winner in a 3-2 success in a friendly at the Owls' ground in August 1994. Earlier in the latter game, Nathan Blake had scored twice for the Blades and Chris Bart-Williams and Ian Taylor had hauled Wednesday level.

Wednesday's David Hirst being challenged by United's Brian Gayle when they clashed in a Pontins League game in January 1994 when both were seeking to prove their fitness after injury.

Hillsborough heroes of different generations: Terry Curran (left) talks to Redfern Froggatt. Curran was later to spend a spell with United, and it is often forgotten that Froggatt, that most loyal of Owls and Wednesday's record post-war marksman before Fantham took the honour from him, nearly moved to Bramall Lane in the 1950s.

Derby Day marksmen of the 1990s, Wednesday's David Hirst (left) and United's Brian Deane.

Six-goal Thriller at Bramall Lane

Saturday, 6 November 1909: United 3 Wednesday 3

THE 31st Football League meeting between the Sheffield clubs produced one of the most memorable of derby days at Bramall Lane, where the Blades and the Owls produced a six-goal thriller in which the honours were properly shared.

United led 2-0 after 18 minutes, Wednesday hit back to go 3-2 up early in the second half, and the Lane men salvaged a point with an 80th-minute equaliser.

The Blades, captained by 'pocket Hercules' Bernard Wilkinson from Thorpe Hesley,

got off to a fine start when a rare error by Teddy Davison presented them with a gift as the Owls' goalkeeper allowed a long effort from Darnall product Bill Brelsford to elude his grasp; and, soon afterwards, Jimmy Simmons claimed a second goal.

Sammy Kirkman, a fast and direct winger making his derby debut, reduced Wednesday's arrears with a brilliant display of tenacity and skill, for, on a great solo run, he recovered after colliding with Joe Brooks and dashed past Albert Sturgess before beating goalkeeper Joe Lievesley. The Owls drew level when Harry

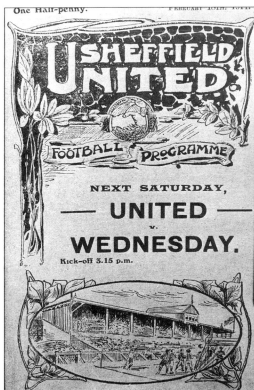

Sheffield United programme from February 1911.

Chapman scored following Andrew Wilson's flick-on from Freddie Foxall's cross.

Seven minutes after the interval, Wednesday claimed the lead with another flash of Kirkman magic. The man

22

This Wednesday team of pre-1914 includes Teddy Davison, the long-serving goalkeeper, David McLean, Teddy Glennon and Andrew Wilson – all derby days heroes.

signed from Carlisle a couple of months earlier showed immaculate control as he collected a dropping ball from a long clearance, then contrived to let the ball bounce once before heading it forward and sweeping past Bob Benson to shoot low into the home net.

Simmons saved the day with a strike ten minutes from the end when he headed in a cross from Bob Evans.

The teams that day were:

United: Lievesley; Benson, Brooks, Brelsford, Wilkinson, Sturgess, Walton, Simmons, Kitchen, Hardinge, Evans.

Wednesday: Davison; Spoors, Holbem, Taylor, McConnell, Brittleton, Kirkman, Chapman, Wilson, Rollinson, Foxall.

When the return game was played at Owlerton the following March, it was

United's turn to come from behind, and on this occasion they went on to win. Tom Brittleton gave Wednesday the lead, but Walter Hardinge equalised and then shot the Blades into a 2-1 lead. Later Evans made it 3-1 and a sad day for the Owls was compounded when Walter Holbem was sent off for kicking Arthur Robins.

'Honest Ted' – A Derby Day George Washington!

TEDDY Davison, Wednesday's goalkeeper in 424 games between 1908 and 1926 and United's manager from 1932 to 1952, had a remarkable derby record in his unique career in Sheffield football. As a player he figured in 11 League derbies and never finished on the losing side; and in his time as boss at Bramall Lane he was involved in 12 derby games and lost only three.

In fact, when he made his senior debut for the Owls in 1908 it was in a charity match with the Blades, and at the end of a game which ended scoreless he had the rare distinction of collecting a medal. But the derby duel with which his name will always be synonymous came on 4 November 1911 in a First Division game which ended 1-1 at Bramall Lane.

Wednesday led through an Andrew Wilson goal, and it was the circumstances of United's

late equaliser, from Joe Kitchen,

which prompted Davison to display the only public outburst of anger recorded in his long career. When the ball went into the net and the referee signalled a goal, the little goalkeeper dashed after the official and insisted United's centre-forward had 'scored' by using an arm.

The pleas fell on deaf ears and the goal stood, but someone who knew Davison went on record as saying: "If he says Joe used an arm, it must have been so, for Teddy is incapable to telling a lie."

On the following Monday an anonymous postcard arrived at the Wednesday ground. It was addressed to: "George Washington, Owlerton". Nobody needed to be told for whom it was intended!

Epic Cup Triumph for United's Mudlarks

Saturday, 31 January 1925: United 3 Wednesday 2

WHEN United won the FA Cup in 1925, Wednesday, then in the Second Division, were one of their victims on the route to Wembley, and this second-round tie, played in ankle-deep mud and continuous rain, has passed into Sheffield football history as one of the most memorable in the long series of city derbies.

A 40,256 Bramall Lane crowd saw Jimmy Trotter score

twice for the Owls in the first nine minutes as the boys from Hillsborough revelled in the benefits of attacking the Shoreham Street goal with the wind and rain on their backs. Wednesday skipper George Wilson had begun the move that led to the first strike, and 'Darkie' Lowdell set up Trotter's second.

But United in the 1920s were not dubbed 'the mudlarks' without good cause,

George Green, who scored a crucial goal in the Cup duel with Wednesday. United's run to Wembley led to him gaining the attention of the England selectors and collecting his first cap at the end of the season.

Tom Sampy's goal inspired a famous United recovery and he went on to strike at the double as the Blades triumphed over the Owls in the 1925 Cup run.

and, overcoming the handicap of appalling conditions and a two-goal deficit, they bounced back in style to haul themselves level by the 20th minute. First Tommy Sampy reduced arrears when a centre from home captain Billy Gillespie was deflected into his path; and then, after Gillespie had

Harold Pantling, a tough United defender of the 1920s.

hit a post, George Green atoned for the error which had led to Wednesday's second goal by grabbing an equaliser.

Conditions were such that referee W.E.Russell from Swindon instructed the teams to forsake a half-time break and turn straight round at the end of the first 45 minutes.

The second half was barely 90 seconds old when Sampy, taking a pass from Harry Johnson and scoring from an awkward angle, emerged the match-winner by

A United team group of the 1920s which features such heroes as legendary skipper Billy Gillespie, Fred Tunstall and Harry Johnson.

Jimmy Trotter, scored twice in first nine minutes for Owls in the Bramall Lane mud before United hit back in the 1925 Cup clash.

shooting the Blades into a lead they refused to relinquish. Ironically, when United finally made it to Wembley at the end of the Cup run, Sampy missed out on the final glory. He was dropped!

The teams were:

United: Sutcliffe; Cook, Birks, Pantling, King, Green, Mercer, Sampy, Johnson, Gillespie, Tunstall.

Wednesday: Brown; Inglis, Felton, Toone, Wilson, Powell, Lowdell, Hill, Trotter, Taylor, Richardson.

The First 'Division One' Derbies of the 1920s

Hillsborough, 26 August 1926: Wednesday 2 United 3

Bramall Lane, 15 January 1927: United 2 Wednesday 0

SHOCK FOR SHEFFIELD UNITED AT HILLSBOROUGH.

HOW THE WEDNESDAY MEN CREATED THE SURPRISE OF THE DAY.

By "Centre-Forward."

Wednesday 2, Sheffield United 1. The Wednesday team surprised friends and foes alike on Saturday in beating their neighbours, Sheffield United. Previously this season they had not won a match, and nothing in the form they had shown suggested the likelihood of their overcoming a smart Bramall lane combination, who, only a week ago, had triumphed over Middlesbro' by 5 goals to 1.

But once again, as they have often done in the past, "the blue and white brigade" a grey occasion, League form is

by him into the net. Thus were the scores made equal 27 minutes after the start, and so they remained up to half time.

The Winning Goal.

Two minutes after change of end Wednesday gained the lead. Cooper getting away on the loft, centred well. Brittleton, with a clean opening before him, failed to gather the ball, but it went across to the right and

IN THE famous 1925 FA Cup duel between the Sheffield clubs, Wednesday centre-forward Jimmy Trotter had the misfortune to score the game's first two goals but still finish on the losing side and, when he again struck at the double to give the Owls the lead after League derbies were resumed at the start of the 1926-27

season, he suffered the same misfortune as United claimed another dramatic victory.

The Blades and the newly-promoted Owls met at Hillsborough in August 1926 in the first League derby at the ground since Campbell and Gill had given the Owls a shock 2-1 win in September 1919. The

game was only three minutes old when the 43,282 crowd saw Wednesday goalkeeper Jack Brown fumble a shot from Freddie Tunstall and allow Harry Johnson to pounce and score. However, Trotter snatched the equaliser a few minutes before half-time. Then, 17 minutes after the interval, Trotter was on hand to shoot

Another Musical Interlude

Bramall Lane, September 1927

When the Sheffield teams shared a 1-1 draw at Bramall Lane in their first Division One meeting of 1927-28, a memorable derby duel was again marked by a pre-match display of vintage community singing. The stars were the legendary Sir Henry Coward, the Sheffield Musical Union choir and the 45,512 crowd.

The game was a full-blooded affair in which Freddie Tunstall shot the Blades in front with a terrific volley at the end of a 50-yard run in which he only touched the ball twice; then Jimmy Trotter pulled the Owls level with a typical opportunist strike.

Wednesday in front following a Burridge free-kick.

United claimed the points with two goals in a three-minute spell in the final seven minutes of the game. First Johnson and skipper Billy Gillespie combined to create a chance which Wally Hoyland seized upon, then Johnson

How Middleton, the cartoonist, saw the first Division One derby of the 1920s, in August 1926.

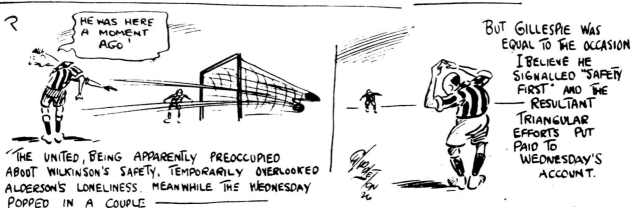

Sheffield Wednesday 1926. Back row (left to right): Kean, Lowdell, Felton, Brown, Froggatt, Blenkinsop, Marsden. Front row: Williams, Barrass, Trotter, Hill, Prince.

grabbed the 85th-minute winner with a first-time effort following a typical run and cross down the left by Tunstall. Wednesday's consolation was that young winger Jack Wilkinson was the 'man of the match'.

The teams were:

Wednesday: Brown; Walker, Blenkinsop; Kean, Froggatt, Burridge; Williams, Anstiss, Trotter, Marsden, Jack Wilkinson.

United: Alderson; Harris, Birks; Tom Sampy, King, Green; David Mercer, Hoyland, Johnson, Gillespie, Tunstall.

The return game on a sunny afternoon in January 1927 was the famous occasion when a

Sir Henry Coward made Bramall Lane derbies extra special occasions leading the fans in pre-match community singing.

60,084 Bramall Lane crowd enjoyed community singing ahead of the football for the first time, with Sir Henry Coward conducting the Imperial

Jimmy Seed – so close to putting the 'lost' ball into the net in the 1928 FA Cup meeting.

Band and the Orpheus Choir. It created a terrific atmosphere, and the match itself was a feast – although ultimately less enjoyable for Owls' fans.

Little Harry Johnson set up United's first goal for Tunstall after 32 minutes with a great run down the middle and a driven diagonal pass which the famous Blades winger met first time as he powered in from the left flank. Arthur Mercer scrambled the second goal in a 2-0 win four minutes from the end.

Teams:

United: Alderson; Harris, Birks, Boyle, King, Green, D.Mercer, A.Mercer, Johnson, Gillespie, Tunstall.

Wednesday: Brown; Walker, Blenkinsop, Lowdell, Kean, Marsden, Rees Williams, Kirkwood, Trotter, Hill, Wilkinson.

Programme for the first Second Division meeting of the clubs in October 1937, when United went to Hillsborough and won 1-0 with a goal from Arthur Eggleston in a duel watched by a 52,523 crowd.

Bert Partridge equalised for United in the first of the 1928 Cup duels, and it set up the famous replay in which Harry Johnson scored a hat-trick.

The Famous 'Lost Ball' Incident

Hillsborough, 18 February 1928

WHEN the Sheffield clubs were paired in the FA Cup fifth round in 1928, the Owls were again knocked off the Wembley trail as the Blades romped to a 4-1 replay triumph at Bramall Lane on the day Harry Johnson claimed an historic derby hat-trick.

However, Wednesday were within inches of winning the first game, at Hillsborough, when their captain, the legendary Jimmy Seed was at the centre of the 'lost ball' incident which has passed into the folklore of local football.

At the time of this game, Wednesday were in the middle of a great (and ultimately successful) battle to avoid relegation from the First Division, but a 57,076 crowd turned up to see them take the lead three minutes after half-time when Strange and Harper combined to set up a chance which winger Jack Wilkinson turned into a goal with a glorious drive. However, within four minutes Bert Partridge grabbed an equaliser after some good work by Gillespie.

It was 12 minutes from the end that the 'lost ball' incident occurred. Following a Mark Hooper corner at the Leppings Lane end, the ball fell loose, and Seed hammered a shot which United goalkeeper Jack Alderson contrived to block with his body. The ball flew into the air – and disappeared! For perhaps 20 seconds nobody seemed to know where it had gone, but, suddenly, the crowd behind the goal spotted it stuck in the mud – barely six inches from the line and slap bang in the middle of the six-yard box.

The ball only needed the slightest touch to put it into the net, and, astonishingly, Seed, standing with his back to the goal, was almost touching it with his heels. Alas, the Owls forward was looking everywhere but in the right place; and the first player to spot the ball was United back Len Birks, who rushed across the goalmouth to belt it to safety.

United survived to reach the semi-final that year before losing to Huddersfield in a marathon tie.

The teams in the 1928 Cup meetings were:

Wednesday: Brown; Walker, Blenkinsop, Smith, Kean, Marsden, Hooper, Strange, Harper, Seed, Wilkinson.

United: Alderson; Chandler, Birks, Sampy, Matthews, Green, Partridge, Blair, Johnson, Gillespie, Tunstall.

Sheffield Wednesday's 1935 Cup winning team. Back row (left to right): Irwin (trainer), Sharp, Nibloe, Brown, Catlin, Millership, Burrows, W.H. Walker (manager). Front row: Hooper, Surtees, Palethorpe, Starling, Rimmer. At the time of this triumph, the Owls and the Blades were in different grades, but they met in April 1935 in a benefit match for the dependents of trainer Chris Craig. The game ended without any goals and attracted only 1,200 spectators. The clubs did not meet in a major derby between the famous occasion in 1934 (when Bill Boyd scored three in a 5-1 Blades victory) and October 1937 when both clubs met in the Second Division for the first time.

Sheffield United's squad in their 1936 Cup Final year. Back row (left to right): J.E. Davison (manager), Jackson, Cox, Smith, Hooper, Wilkinson, McPherson, D. Steele (trainer). Front row: Barton, Williams, Barclay, Stacey, Dodds, Pickering, Bird, T. Johnson, Boot.

Some Derby Day Personalities

BOB EVANS, the man with the unique record of having been capped by both Wales and England, made his farewell appearance for United in a derby fixture at Bramall Lane on Boxing Day 1918 when goals from Utley, Kitchen and Brown gave the Blades a 3-0 victory.

HAROLD GOUGH, the goalkeeper United banned after he broke a club rule by taking over a public house, made his last appearance for the Blades in a County Cup Final at Hillsborough on 10 May 1924 when goals from Billy Gillespie and Harry Johnson sent the Owls to defeat.

WALTER SPICER was best known as a Sheffield United cricketer, but he made his senior debut as a Blades footballer in the County Cup semi-final with Wednesday at Hillsborough in November 1930.

CHARLIE WILKINSON, a full-back who joined United from Leeds, made his Blades debut in a First Division game against Wednesday at Hillsborough in October 1933 when the Owls were defeated 1-0 with a goal from Bert Williams.

DAVID STEELE, a former Scottish international and United's coach in the 1930s, made his only appearance in a Blades' team when he turned out in the Sheffield derby match arranged to raise funds for the family of former Owls' trainer Chris Craig at Hillsborough in April 1935.

JACKIE MILBURN, the legendary goal-scoring Newcastle United forward, made one guest appearance for the Blades in a League North wartime game which also doubled as a County Cup match in which Wednesday provided the opposition at

Hillsborough on 26 May 1945.

PETER SHILTON, the famous England goalkeeper, was with Leicester City when he guested for Wednesday in Len Badger's testimonial match at Bramall Lane on 20 March 1973.

HERBERT CHAPMAN, who earned fame as the legendary manager of Huddersfield and Arsenal, joined Sheffield United in 1902

and made his Blades debut in the First Division derby game with Wednesday at Bramall Lane in September of that year. His younger brother, Harry Chapman, was playing for the Owls.

BARRY BUTLER, who came into Wednesday's side in January 1954 after Ralph O'Donnell broke his leg, was thrust into derby day action in only his second and third senior games in the famous FA Cup third-round duels of that year. Ivor Seemley was also having only his third senior outing when he faced the Blades at Hillsborough.

BRIAN RYALLS was 20 and had played in only six reserve games when he was called up to make his First Division debut for the Owls in the derby match against United at Bramall Lane in September 1953. Less than a year earlier he had been playing with Grimethorpe Colliery in the

Sheffield Association League. The first goal he conceded in his senior career was scored by Jimmy Hagan – at the second attempt after the young goalkeeper had pushed the first effort straight back to the legendary Blades hero.

The picture at top of page was taken at Hillsborough on 25 April 1970 and features Don Megson and Harold Wilcockson, the Wednesday defenders, combating the threat of United's John Tudor in the Gerry Young testimonial derby. A crowd of 12,120 saw Jack Whitham (2) and Alan Warboys score for the Owls, with Billy Dearden, Tony Currie and David Staniforth on target for the Blades in a 3-3 draw.

JOHN BARNWELL is seen here making his Blades debut in

the Gerry Young testimonial, and Dearden was also a newcomer in the United side that day. Dearden was to figure in the Second Division derby duels of 1970-71, but Barnwell never played in a 'major' Sheffield derby.

LAWRIE MADDEN'S testimonial game between the

Owls and the Blades in August 1990 marked the arrival in the Wednesday team of newcomers Paul Williams and Danny Wilson, while United also had a new boy in John Pemberton. Williams scored twice and Peter Shirtliff also found the net as Wednesday won 3-0 to lift the new Sheffield Steel Cup. Our picture shows Madden (right) and United skipper Paul Stancliffe with their sons before the match.

England inside forwards who wore the Owls' blue-and-white, Ronnie Starling (left) and 'Red' Froggatt. Starling played in four League derbies between September 1932 and

March 1934. Froggatt's first League derby was in September 1949, his last in October 1958.

The Springett brothers, Peter (left) and Ron, both played in Sheffield derby games for Wednesday, but while Ron figured in 13 in League and

Cup between 1958 and 1966, Peter played in only two, both in the 1967-68 campaign.

ERNEST BLENKINSOP (right) played in 13 League derbies between 1926 and 1933, and was usually partnered by Tommy Walker. Here he is seen in conversation with his deputy and ultimate successor at left-back in the Owls team, Ted Catlin, who figured in three League derbies and had a different partner in each – Beeson, Walker and Ashley.

TOMMY HOYLAND was on the winning side in his three League derbies with United in the 1950s. He became a publican, and below he displays a picture of the Blades side in which he was a favourite.

TOM JOHNSON made his derby debut with United in October 1937 when the Sheffield clubs met for the first time in the Second Division. He played in four pre-war League derbies and was on the losing side only once.

JAMIE HOYLAND emulated his father by playing for the Blades against the Owls after arriving from Bury.

Like father, like son; Jamie Hoyland joined United to emulate his father in the fixture.

Wartime Derbies

THE biggest attendance at a Sheffield derby in wartime was 43,718 to watch a goalless draw at Bramall Lane on 10 April 1943. The first wartime meeting was at Hillsborough on 2 December 1939 when a 5,500 crowd saw United win 3-2 with goals from John Sheen, Colin Collindridge and Edgar Packard (the latter putting the ball in his own net).

A wartime game of special interest was the derby match staged to celebrate VE Day on 9 May 1945. It was played at Bramall Lane, where a 15,045 crowd paid receipts of £1,072 8s 7d, and United won 2-0 with goals from Jack Pickering and Bower. The line-up was:

United: White; Furniss, G.Shephard, H.Shepherd, Latham, Jackson, Dale, Nightingale, Forbes, J.Pickering, Bower.

Wednesday: Gadsby; Swift, Bill Pickering, Ward, Turton, Cockroft, Bates, Rogers, Lindsay, Froggatt, Tomlinson.

WELL ON TARGET

SHEFFIELD WEDNESD
SCORE EIGHT

Sheffield Wednesday 8, Sheff
United 2.

Defeating Sheffield United 8—2 at Hillsborough, a re score for these local ri heffield Wednesday took h ome revenge for their 3—1 d t Bramall Lane last week.

Their spirit in the first half nost marked and after Robinso cored the opening goal afte minutes' play, the United defe ollapsed completely.

Hesitant clearances and overing by United's defence s Vednesday through time afte tir and goal quickly. T W esday

The first Christmas Day meeting of the Sheffield clubs in the war was a friendly at Bramall Lane in 1939 when United won 2-1 with goals from John Sheen and Alf Jeffries (pen).

SHEFFIELD UNITED

VERSUS

SHEFFIELD WEDNESDAY

MONDAY, 25th DECEMBER, 1939.
KICK-OFF 11.0 A.M.

NEXT HOME MATCH
Saturday, 30th December, 1939 (2.15 p.m.)
LEEDS UNITED

OFFICIAL PROGRAMME ONE PENNY

Albert Nightingale, a Blades wartime hero.

Frank Melling, who was on target in the Owls' 8-2 win. He later became a Blades director.

Jackie Robinson, a hat-trick hero in the 8-2 defeat of United in 1943.

Programme of the famous wartime game in 1943 when Wednesday won 8-2 with goals from Robinson (3), Melling (2), Jack Thompson (2) and Reynolds.

A Sheffield Derby in the Isle of Man

Whit Monday, 17 May 1948: United 2 Wednesday 2

HISTORY was made when a Whitsuntide holiday crowd of around 8,000 in the King George V Park in Douglas, Isle of Man, witnessed the first post-war Sheffield derby and the first match between the Blades and the Owls staged outside the city of steel. It was also the first time two Football League clubs had sent teams to the island to play each other.

The game ended all square. Eddie Quigley gave Wednesday the lead after ten minutes from Jackie Marriott's centre, but early in the second half Colin Collindridge equalised for United and then Paddy Sloan

Wednesday centre-half Cyril Turton. He played in the Isle of Man game. Turton's only appearance in a League derby was in the Bramall Lane game of 1951, when the Owls lost 7-3.

put them in front. However, Quigley notched his second goal after 80 minutes to make the final scoreline 2-2.

With the Blades in Division One and the Owls in Division Two, the absence of a local derby from the football calendar was a source of frustration to many, and this unique fixture came about when the Sheffield firm, Hope & Anchor, established links with the Castletown Brewery on the Isle of Man. The football connection was provided by brothers Tom and Chris Carter, one a United director and the other on the Wednesday board; both being attached to Hope & Anchor Breweries.

For the record, musical entertainment was provided by the Castletown Metropolitan Band and the Army Cadet Force Band; and the referee was the famous Liverpool official W.H. 'Bill' Evans, who

Goalkeeper Fred White (right), pictured here with Alan Hodgkinson, another Blades' hero in green, never played in a League or Cup derby, but he had the distinction of figuring in the unique game on the Isle of Man. He later played in the famous 4-2 defeat of the Owls in the County Cup in February 1949.

ISLE OF MAN FOOTBALL ASSOCIATION

Under the Distinguished Patronage of His Excellency
the Lieut.-Governor, Air Vice-Marshal Sir Geoffrey
Bromet, K.B.E., C.B., D.S.O.

By permission of the F.A.

SHEFFIELD UNITED
v.
SHEFFIELD WEDNESDAY
at
King George V Park
DOUGLAS, ISLE OF MAN
WHIT MONDAY, MAY 17th, 1948

Kick-Off 3.30 p.m.

Souvenir Programme

Programme for the 1948 Isle of Man Sheffield derby.

later spent many years as a Wednesday scout.

The teams that day were:
United: Fred White; Fred Furniss, Albert Cox, Dick Young, Harry Latham, Harold Brook, Dennis Thompson, Paddy Sloan, Colin Collindridge, Jimmy Hagan (captain), George Jones.
Wednesday: Dave McIntosh; Frank Westlake, Hugh Swift, Doug Witcomb (captain), Cyril Turton, Keith Bannister, Jackie Marriott, Eddie Quigley, Clarrie Jordan, Redfern Froggatt, Dennis Woodhead.

Blades 'Breeze' to a County Cup Triumph

Hillsborough: Saturday 12 February 1949

THE first post-war Sheffield derby on home soil was a County Cup semi-final which attracted a 49,980 crowd (a record for the competition) to Hillsborough – and they saw United, who won 4-2, profit from Wednesday's failure to ignore tradition and adapt to the circumstances of the day.

It was the Owls' custom to kick uphill towards the Leppings Lane end in the first half whenever they won the toss, and this is what skipper Eddie Quigley chose to do – despite an exceedingly strong wind blowing downfield toward the Kop.

'It was a grave error of judgement', wrote Fred Walters, the doyen of Sheffield sportswriters, in *The Star*. 'United,

The Sheffield and Hallamshire County Cup. United were the first winners of this trophy in May 1921 when goals from Harry Johnson and Albert Rawson earned them a 2-1 victory over Wednesday in the final at Hillsborough in front of an attendance of 21,203.

Eddie Quigley, the Owls' skipper boobed in choosing to kick against the wind, and two second-half goals were not enough to save Wednesday from defeat in February 1949. However, he helped the Owls to a League victory over the Blades in the following September.

who included four reserves, exploited the conditions for all they were worth in the first-

half, and were four goals to the good by the interval.'

George Hutchinson set the

Blades on their way when he scored after 24 minutes, and Jimmy Hagan claimed a second

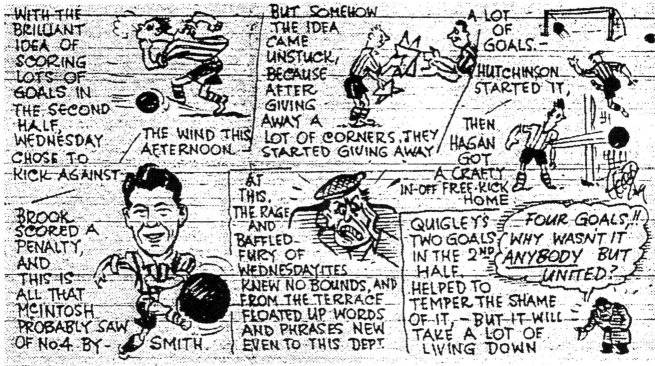

WITH THE BRILLIANT IDEA OF SCORING LOTS OF GOALS IN THE SECOND HALF, WEDNESDAY CHOSE TO KICK AGAINST —

THE WIND THIS AFTERNOON.

BUT SOMEHOW THE IDEA CAME UNSTUCK, BECAUSE AFTER GIVING AWAY A LOT OF CORNERS, THEY STARTED GIVING AWAY —

A LOT OF GOALS. — HUTCHINSON STARTED IT, THEN HAGAN GOT A CRAFTY IN-OFF FREE-KICK HOME

BROOK SCORED A PENALTY, AND THIS IS ALL THAT McINTOSH PROBABLY SAW OF No.4 BY — SMITH.

AT THIS, THE RAGE AND BAFFLED FURY OF WEDNESDAYITES KNEW NO BOUNDS, AND FROM THE TERRACE FLOATED UP WORDS AND PHRASES NEW EVEN TO THIS DEPT.

QUIGLEY'S TWO GOALS IN THE 2ND HALF HELPED TO TEMPER THE SHAME OF IT, — BUT IT WILL TAKE A LOT OF LIVING DOWN

FOUR GOALS!! WHY WASN'T IT ANYBODY BUT UNITED?

How cartoonist Harry Heap saw the 1949 County Cup semi-final.

just past the half-hour when his shot-cum-centre took a deflection off an Owls' defender. Then, on 39 minutes home goalkeeper Dave McIntosh brought down winger George Jones and Harold

Brook converted the penalty; and F.E.Smith notched the fourth four minutes before the break

To add to Wednesday's woe, they started the second half without Redfern Froggatt, who retired with a groin strain; and, although

they now had the wind on their backs, somehow it didn't seem quite so strong and the Owls could not manage to do more than halve their deficit.

On the hour Quigley pounced to score after Blades' goalkeeper Fred White and defender Graham Bailey, plus home forward Alf Rogers, all fell in a heap; and the skipper claimed a last-minute consolation from the penalty-spot following a handling offence.

Teams:

Wednesday: McIntosh; Westlake, Swift, Locherty, Turton, Witcomb, Kilshaw, Rogers, Quigley, Froggatt, Woodhead.

United: White; Bailey, Cox, Hitchen, Latham, Joe Shaw, Hutchinson, Hagan, F.E.Smith, Brook, Jones.

Footnotes:

(1) United and Wednesday had previously met in the city on three occasions in the 1945-46

Match programme for the County Cup semi-final of February 1949.

Joe Shaw – the 1949 game gave him his first experience of derby day. He was to play in 17 League derbies, the FA Cup duels of 1954 and 1960, and many other County Cup fixtures between the Sheffield clubs.

Jimmy Hagan was often at his best in derby duels. He played in his first League duel against the Owls as a United man in March 1939 and his last in 1954; and he figured in a few intriguing battles in the County Cup. Wednesday so admired him that they once tried to sign him by offering a then record £32,000 for him. The Blades said yes, but 'Sir Jimmy' rejected the move!

season, when Wednesday completed a hat-trick of wins – two in the Football League North and one in the County Cup. As is noted elsewhere, the first Sheffield derby after the war was staged in the Isle of Man.

(2) It was in September 1949, following United's relegation from Division One, that United and Wednesday resumed their meetings in the Football League, with the Owls winning 2-1 at Hillsborough thanks to goals from Clarrie Jordan and Quigley. Later that same season, in January 1950, United won the return fixture 2-0 with goals from Harold Brook and Roy Warhurst.

1951-52: A Famous Blades Treble

Fred Furniss. In his United career the Sheffield-born full-back only missed two of 20 penalties, and the one superbly saved by Dave McIntosh in September 1951 hardly proved costly for the Blades as they went on to register a record 7-3 win.

September 8: United 7 Wednesday 3

January 5: Wednesday 1 United 3

May 5: Wednesday 1 United 3

WEDNESDAY won the Second Division championship in 1951-52, but United beat them three times that season – twice in the League and finally in the County Cup. It was the year Derek Dooley hit 46 goals but managed only one against the Blades; while Alf Ringstead and Derek Hawksworth each put four into the Owls' net.

United were in a memorable free-scoring run (49 goals in their first 15 matches) when they chalked up a record 7-3 derby triumph before 52,045 spectators at Bramall Lane in September. After an hour the score stood at 2-2: Keith Thomas had put the Owls in front inside 90 seconds and Dennis Woodhead levelled after Hawksworth and Brook had given the Blades the initiative.

Before Woodhead's 60th minute equaliser, United's Fred Furniss had a penalty saved by Dave McIntosh, but then Ringstead (2), Hawksworth and F.A.Smith made it 6-2 with four strikes in 11 minutes. Woodhead reduced arrears on 87 minutes, but Harold Brook got United's seventh just before the end.

Teams:

United: Burgin; Furniss,

Alf Ringstead, the Republic of Ireland international winger struck at the double in both the Second Division derby duels of 1951-52. He figured in seven League derbies, his last in October 1958.

8,000 Turn Up at Central League derby

A derby game of special note was the Central League duel at Bramall Lane in September 1952 when a crowd of over 8,000 turned up to see Derek Dooley, dropped from the senior team, seek to end a miserable and goalless start to his First Division career.

In this match, Dennis Woodhead missed a 30th-minute penalty for the Owls and, almost immediately, Sammy McNab then scored from the spot for the Blades. Brian Slater equalised for Wednesday from a Woodhead centre after half-time, and, finally, in the last five minutes Dooley struck at the double to seal a 3-1 win – prompting cheers which must have been heard across the city at Hillsborough!

United Reserves: Crookes; Coldwell, G.Shaw, Gratton, Denial, Walker, Hudson, Hoyland, Ryan, Turner, McNab.

Wednesday Reserves: Morton; Underwood, Kenny, Edwards, O'Donnell, Davies, Finney, J.McAnearney, Dooley, Slater, Woodhead.

Redfern Froggatt had a 70th-minute penalty saved in the Hillsborough derby of January 1952.

Cox, Hitchen, Latham, J.Shaw, Ringstead, F.A.Smith, Brook, Hagan, Hawksworth.

Wednesday: McIntosh; Jackson, Kenny, Gannon, Turton, Witcomb, Finney, Sewell, Woodhead, Thomas, Rickett.

By the time of the Hillsborough return in January, the fortunes of the teams had changed dramatically. Dooley had finally arrived and scored 27 goals in a 15-match run in which the Owls had lost

only twice; while the Blades had won only two games in 12. Few gave United much chance, but they emerged 3-1 victors as a 65,385 crowd saw Ringstead claim the lead after 20 minutes and, although Dooley levelled almost immediately, second-half goals from Ringstead and Hutchinson sealed the points.

At 2-1 to United, Wednesday missed a 70th-minute penalty conceded by 17-year-old debutant Graham

Dennis Woodhead, the winger who was playing centre-forward when he scored two of the Owls' three goals at Bramall Lane in 1951. Keith Thomas got the other.

Derek Dooley had scored 27 goals in 15 games ahead of the derby of January 1952, and Heap, the cartoonist, suggested United would need to take the Bramall Lane cricket score-board to Hillsborough to keep count of the goals the 'goal kid' was sure to score against the Blades, but the prolific marksman was subdued by Harry Latham and found the target just once.

How Harry Heap, The Star & Green 'Un cartoonist, saw the Hillsborough derby of January 1952

Shaw, with Ted Burgin brilliantly saving Redfern Froggatt's fiercely struck spot-kick. Meanwhile, poor Dooley hardly got a look in: Blades centre-half Harry Latham certainly kept him quiet!

Wednesday: McIntosh; Bannister, Kenny, Gannon, O'Donnell, Davies, Finney, Froggatt, Dooley, Quixall, Marriott.
United: Burgin; Furniss, G.Shaw, Hitchen, Latham, J.Shaw, Ringstead, F.A.Smith, Browning, Brook, Hutchinson.

The Blades completed a hat-trick of wins when they went back to Hillsborough in May and claimed another 3-1 triumph in a County Cup semi-final, with Jimmy Hagan

Harry Latham, a long-serving and loyal servant of Sheffield United who enjoyed one of his finest afternoons on the day he bottled up Dooley.

"having trouble Derek?"

Scodger and the Dooley Bird

You remember that famous battle
Twixt the Blades & the Owls at the Lane
When the Blades did the Owls good & proper
And left them to die in great pain.

The Owl was stuffed in September
But rose from the dead once again
In the form of an odd sort of creature
The Dooley Bird, that was its name.

No one could do much about it
For no one had seen such a thing
And centre-halves tore their hair madly
Some threatened to write to the King

But one little lad named Scodger
Showed not a morsel of fear
When they told him he'd meet it on Saturday
Said "Is that so? Lets have a Beer!"

Some were for pinching the Dooley Birds boots,
Some were for setting a Trap,
They said "If only we had Jimmy back,
He'd know what to do with the chap"

So, on the day of the battle
The Dooleyites were brimful of joy
They'd bragged for weeks beforehand
That Dooley would DO Lathams boy

But Scodger knew his onions
And before you could say three one
He'd tied up that Dooley Bird proper
And I do mean proper my son.

We'd like to warn you Wednesday
There's no such things as certs
And next time we're due at Hillsboro'
We'll only send't Red and White shirts.

C.P. Thornton

How Blades supporter C.P. Thornton honoured 'Scodger' Latham's derby day display.

Wednesday suffered a hat-trick of defeats at the hands of the Blades in 1951-52, but they went on to win the Second Division title. Pictured in this line-up are: Back row (left to right): Sam Powell (trainer), Norman Curtis, Eddie Gannon, Vin Kenny, Cyril Turton, Dave McIntosh, George Davies, Ralph O'Donnell, Dennis Woodhead, Doug Witcomb, Tommy Walker (trainer). Front row: Alan Brown (coach), Redfern Froggatt, Albert Quixall, Derek Dooley, Keith Bannister, Jackie Sewell, Walter Rickett, Alan Finney, Eric Taylor (secretary-manager).

United only had to wait a year before they, too, won the Second Division title and Sheffield derbies were resumed in 1953-54. This 1953 line-up shows: Back row (left to right): Fred Furniss, Joe Shaw, Ted Burgin, Harry Latham, Bill Toner, Graham Shaw. Front row: Reg Freeman (manager), Alf Ringstead, Jimmy Hagan, Len Browning, Harold Brook, Derek Hawksworth, Ernest Jackson (trainer).

scoring after 22 minutes and Hawksworth notching a double before Jackie Marriott hit a consolation goal for the Owls.

It took United only a year to follow Wednesday into the top-grade.

Graham Shaw, the full-back destined to become an England player made his League debut at the age of 17 in the Hillsborough derby of January 1952. Pulled out of the reserve match an hour earlier, he thought he was going to be United's 12th man, but when the players reached the dressing-room manager Teddy Davison told him he was standing in for the injured Albert Cox. Shaw conceded a penalty (which Burgin saved), but it was his only slip on a memorable day. The Southey lad was brought up a Wednesdayite, but, looking back, his only regret about his debut was his late call-up meant he missed the team's traditional pre-match meal at Davy's Café in Fargate!

The FA Cup Duels of 1954

Saturday January 9:
Wednesday 1 United 1

Wednesday January 13:
United 1 Wednesday 3

THERE were four Sheffield derbies in 1953-54. Honours were divided in the first Division One meeting in 19 years, with United winning 2-0 at home in September and Wednesday claiming the points with a 3-2 success in the January return at Hillsborough. However, it was the FA Cup third-round duels in January which earned a special niche in the history of clashes between the teams, for in winning in the replay Wednesday claimed their first triumph at Bramall Lane since February 1933, wartime matches excepted.

You had to go back to 1928

'Mick' Kenny, speaking of the sending off incident in the 1954 FA Cup replay at Bramall Lane, said: "I never touched Hagan. If I had he wouldn't have played for a month! I think Colin Rawson had curled a free-kick towards our goal and, anticipating where the ball was dropping, I got there just before Jimmy, but he fell as if I'd caught him. I couldn't believe it when I was sent off, but you didn't argue in those days. I went straight to the dressing room, which meant I missed seeing the goals that won the game." Someone noted that the 'battle' between Kenny and Hagan had started in the first game when the pair were lectured; and also recalled a free-kick which Hagan had hit straight at Kenny (leaving him doubled up in pain) when the Owls back failed to retreat.

for the last time the clubs had met in the FA Cup, and Wednesday had never beaten their city rivals in the competition. True to that pattern, in front of a 61,250 Hillsborough crowd United took the lead after 30 minutes when a magical Jimmy Hagan run ended with the Blades idol hitting a post before Bill Toner

scored from the rebound. It took the Owls until a minute after half-time to get the goal which led to a replay, Jack Shaw finding the net at the Kop end after Alan Finney and Jackie Sewell had created the opening.

Despite the absence of injured skipper Harold Brook in the Lane replay, United were

Goalmouth action in the Hillsborough derby of 1954 as United's goalkeeper collects the ball at the Leppings Lane End, with Wednesday's Jack Shaw challenging and Blades defender Howard Johnson looking on.

George Davies, the half-back signed from Oswestry scored only two goals in 109 games for the Owls, and his first was the one which set Wednesday on the way to a famous derby victory at Bramall Lane in the 1954 FA Cup replay.

Howard Johnson, a centre-half who played for the Inland Revenue before United tried him out with Norton Woodseats. He played in all four Sheffield derbies in 1953-54 and they were his only senior outings against the Owls.

Jack Shaw, a close-season signing from Rotherham who scored 27 goals for Wednesday. He got the equaliser in the Hillsborough FA Cup game and a fortnight later scored two in the Owls' 3-2 home First Division defeat of the Blades to launch one of his best runs in his time with the club.

still firm favourites, and their early domination hinted at another success. True, in a blizzard of snow they wasted abundant chances, including a ninth-minute penalty which Toner shot straight at Brian Ryalls, the 21-year-old who had made his League debut in the September meeting of the teams.

The breakthrough finally came eight minutes before half-time when Ryalls let Derek Hawksworth's 25-yard effort slip past him; but on 53 minutes Alan Finney equalised for Wednesday – and that was when the fireworks started.

The game got so rough that referee Jack Clough called together rival skippers Joe Shaw and Jackie Sewell and told them to instruct their men to cool down. Alas, that didn't happen, and, in the 62nd minute, Wednesday back Vin (he was always known as 'Mick') Kenny was sent off after a clash with Hagan.

(It is worth noting that the

Jackie Sewell, the Owls' skipper who sealed a famous Wednesday victory three minutes from the end of the Bramall Lane Cup battle.

League meeting of the previous September had passed into the records as 'Hagan's match', and the memory of that marvellous display had ensured the Owls didn't need reminding of the threat he posed. 'Sir Jimmy' was often the target of tough treatment in his career, but he could also look after himself!)

Remarkably, being reduced to ten men brought out the best in the Owls, and first George Davies cracked a superb 25-yard shot past Ted Burgin in the 80th minute (it was his first senior goal), then Sewell sealed victory with

Harold Brook, the Blades skipper, missed the 1954 Cup replay through injury, but scored two when the teams renewed their rivalry in the First Division later in the same month.

another strike three minutes before the final whistle. Wednesday went on to reach the semi-final that year.

Teams in the Cup derbies:
Wednesday: Ryalls; Kenny, Seemley, Gannon, Butler, Davies, Finney, Quixall, Shaw, Sewell, Woodhead.
United: Burgin; Coldwell, Ridge, Shaw, Johnson, Rawson, Ringstead, Hagan, Toner, Brook*, Hawksworth.
*Replaced by Peter Wragg in the replay.

A duel between United's Howard Johnson and Wednesday's Jackie Marriott in the League derby of 1953. The crowd at Bramall Lane that day was 45,463, and they saw goals from Hagan and Hawksworth seal a home victory.

Jimmy Hagan turned in a memorable display in the First Division derby between the Sheffield clubs at Bramall Lane in September 1953, and was involved in the build-up to United's goal in the first Cup match. The Owls were keen to subdue his threat in the replay, and 'Mick' Kenny had the misfortune to be sent off following a clash with the Lane idol.

Action from 1954 as this Sheffield United shot crashes against the bar.

The Secret Sheffield Derby

WHEN the Owls and the Blades met for the first time under floodlights at Hillsborough in the autumn of 1955, the match was played behind closed doors and was supposed to be a private affair in which the 30 or so privileged spectators were sworn to keep the details of the game secret. The hundreds who viewed the novel scene from the nearby hillside had little idea of the outcome of an historic event.

"I can't tell you of the match or the remarkable result," wrote 'Monty' Marston in the next morning's *Sheffield Telegraph*. "It was my understanding with Wednesday secretary-manager Eric Taylor that for the privilege of being present I should disclose no details of this practice match."

However, while the local Press honoured the request from the clubs, the national media ensured the world soon knew that Wednesday had won 7-2 with hat-tricks from Jackie Sewell and Roy Shiner and a goal from Albert Quixall. United's reply had come from Alf Ringstead and a Peter Wragg penalty.

The idea of the match was to help both teams get

'Monty' Marston, one of the most respected football writers on the local scene in the early post-war era, reported on the 'secret' match of October 1955 in the Sheffield Telegraph.

I WATCHED THIS SECRET MATCH
But must not tell shock result

I WAS one of 30 or so privileged people who saw Sheffield Wednesday play Sheffield United under floodlights at Hillsborough last night, but it is with regret that I cannot tell you of the match, or the remarkable result.

It was my understanding with Wednesday secretary-manager Eric Taylor that for the privilege of being present I should disclose no details of this practice match which...

Tommy Hoyland, on target in the County Cup game of November 1955 when the Blades avenged that hefty 'secret' defeat.

experience of what was then a new development which was clearly going to revolutionise the game – floodlit football. Wednesday had played their first match under lights in this country at Derby in November 1953, and their own equipment had been formally launched when the Derek Dooley benefit was staged at Hillsborough in March 1955.

United's first floodlit fixture at Bramall Lane had been against Rotherham in March 1954, and they subsequently entertained some foreign opponents.

Now the Owls were set to entertain Hungarian Cup holders, Vasas of Budapest within the week, and, as several players had never played under lights, this game with United offered an opportunity for practice not to be missed. In the event, when the Hungar-

Roy Shiner, scored a hat-trick in the 'secret' derby game of 1955.

ians came it was they who provided all the dazzle as they beat Wednesday 7-1 before a staggering 45,983 crowd.

Teams in the 'secret' derby were:

Wednesday: McIntosh; Staniforth, Bingley, Gibson, McEvoy, Kay (T.McAnearney 45), Froggatt, Sewell, Shiner, Quixall, Broadbent.

United: Thompson; Coldwell, Mason, Hoyland, J.Shaw, Iley, Ringstead, Howitt, Wragg, Rawson, Grainger.

The referee was George McCabe, the Sheffield official who spent 17 years on the Football League and was ten years on the FIFA list. After his retirement, George worked for the Owls for many years and later took up an appointment at Bramall Lane.

Incidentally, United soon avenged that 7-2 defeat, for, within a month, on 2 November, they returned to Hillsborough to thrash the Owls 5-2 in a County Cup-tie. This time Ringstead claimed a double and Wragg, Jimmy Hagan and Tommy Hoyland were on target. Wednesday came from behind to lead 2-1 after 48 minutes with goals from Froggatt and Shiner, but it was Blades' fans in the 16,158 crowd who went home celebrating.

Blades Out of Luck: FA Cup 1960

Bramall Lane, 12 March 1960: United 0 Wednesday 2

THE FA Cup quarter-final of 1960 was the Sheffield derby in which Wednesday enjoyed so much good fortune they felt sure they were destined to go all the way to Wembley and win the game's most coveted trophy.

Ron Springett, the Owls' England goalkeeper, recalled: "I think we only got into United's half twice all through the game, but on each occasion Derek Wilkinson scored. It was just as if we were fated to win, and the United lads could justly claim they were robbed.

"United threw everything at us, and how they didn't score I'll never know. It was one of those days when every shot I

A 59,692 crowd saw the Sheffield teams meet in the FA Cup quarter-final in 1960, and the match programme notes that Bramall Lane now had 'accommodation for 35,000 under cover'.

had to deal with seemed to stick in my hands – even when I was standing on my head!"

This was the day when a temporary stand erected in

Derek Wilkinson – his goals gave Wednesday victory.

front of the old cricket pavilion provided 3,200 extra seats and a 59,692 Bramall Lane crowd

Alan Hodgkinson played in 18 League and one FA Cup derby in an outstanding career as United's goalkeeper.

Action from the 75th League derby at Bramall Lane in September 1961, when United won 1-0 with a late strike from 'Doc' Pace (seen here diving at the ball with his hand up) in a game remembered as the one in which referee Kevin Howley asked Wednesday to wear white shorts instead of black ones after half-time. Also in this picture are Keith Kettleborough (10) and Owls defenders Don Megson and Peter Swan.

saw Second Division United produce 14 shots on target to First Division Wednesday's six in Sheffield's 187th derby. The Blades also totted up twice as many corners as the Owls (12 to 5); but they simply could not convert greater possession into goals.

Wilkinson settled the issue with strikes after nine and 34 minutes, but when Wednesday went through to the semi-final they lost to Blackburn at Maine Road. They had used up all their luck at Bramall Lane!

Incidentally, Springett played in 13 derbies in League and Cup between 1958 and 1966 and was a winner on four of these occasions. Derek Pace and Alan Birchenall each scored six League goals against the man who for many years was Wednesday's most-capped international.

Tickets for the 1960 FA Cup derby were in heavy demand, but this one, which cost 2s 6d and was for the Spion Kop at Bramall Lane, was never used by author Keith Farnsworth. He explains: "I didn't get my hands on it until it was too late to get to the game. At the time the tickets went on

sale, strange as it might seem 35 years later, I didn't have the ready money to buy one. After they had all been sold, someone promised to get me one, but it didn't arrive in my hands until nearly four o'clock, and by the time I could have made it to the ground the match would have been over. But I kept it as a souvenir of a famous derby I missed out on!"

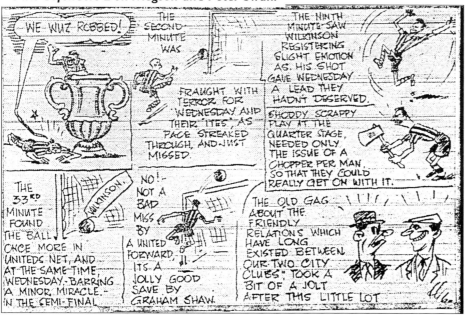

How Harry Heap saw the 1960 FA Cup clash.

Duel in the sun... Ron Springett leaves his goal at the Bramall Lane End to beat United's Keith Kettleborough to the ball, with Megson looking on, in the derby game of October 1962.

Ron Springett, the Wednesday goalkeeper, is grounded after making a save, with colleague Megson and United's Pace on the scene.

Heap's cartoon of the September 1963 derby at Bramall Lane, which ended 1-1, with Simpson scoring for United and Finney equalising for Wednesday

How cartoonist Heap captured the derby duel of January 1964 when Wednesday won 3-0 at Hillsborough with goals from Wilkinson (2) and Layne.

United's former England goalkeeper Alan Hodgkinson, who made his derby debut in September 1954, played in 18 League games against the Owls and just the once in the FA Cup. His last League derby was in the 3-2 victory at Bramall Lane in October 1970.

The 1960 Cup teams were:

United: Hodgkinson; Coldwell, G.Shaw, Richardson, J.Shaw, Summers, Lewis, Hamilton, Pace, Hodgson, Simpson.

Wednesday: Springett; Martin, Megson, McAnearney, Swan, Kay, Wilkinson, Craig, Ellis, Fantham, Finney.

Referee: J.Kelly (Chorley).

The famous occasion of September 1964 when United went to Hillsborough and won 2-0 with goals from teenager Alan Birchenall (right), who marked his derby debut, and only his second Football League outing, with a memorable double. Here Owls goalkeeper Ron Springett collects a high cross, with Vic Mobley looking on.

The 200th Sheffield Derby

Saturday, 24 September 1966: Wednesday 2 United 2

A 43,557 crowd at Hillsborough for the 200th game between the Sheffield clubs included Alf Ramsey on his first visit to a match in the city since leading England to their famous 1966 World Cup triumph the previous summer – and he could not deny the teams served up an entertaining duel. United, who lost Bernard Shaw with an ankle injury early in the game, were two goals ahead after only 19 minutes, but Wednesday hit back to salvage a point in the 85th League meeting of the Owls and Blades since 1893.

Gil Reece provided the cross from which Alan Woodward scored after seven minutes, and

Programme for the 200th Sheffield derby.

Len Badger was the provider when Mick Jones seized on a centre which rebounded off Sam Ellis as the Blades went 2-0 up.

The Owls pulled a goal back five minutes before half-time when John Fantham hammered a free-kick against United's defensive wall and the ball was deflected past goalkeeper Alan Hodgkinson off the ankle of substitute David Munks; and, in the 67th minute, Jim McCalliog celebrated his derby debut with an equaliser which followed a fine run down the left flank by home skipper Don Megson.

OFFICIAL PROGRAMME   PRICE 6d

SHEFFIELD WEDNESDAY

versus SHEFFIELD UNITED

ON SATURDAY, 24th SEPTEMBER, 1966.   KICK-OFF 3.0 P.M.

LEAGUE DIVISION ONE FOOTBALL AT *Hillsborough*

In the 199th Sheffield derby, in March 1966, Alan Birchenall (left), seen here winning a chase with Owls' skipper Don Megson, scored two goals for the second time, but on this occasion the game ended with honours shared as Fantham and Eustace scored for Wednesday. Of interest in this picture is evidence of redevelopment of the Leppings Lane End of Hillsborough in preparation for the World Cup matches.

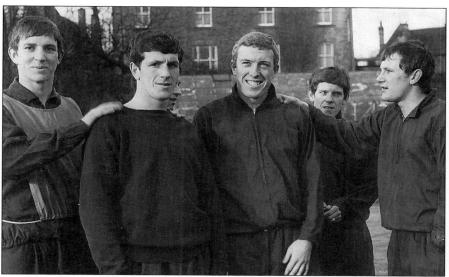

United's young derby stars of the late 1960s (left to right): Mick Hill, Alan Woodward, Mick Jones, Bernard Shaw and Len Badger.

Below: Cec Coldwell, who made his derby debut in the famous FA Cup games of 1954, totted up a dozen appearances in League and Cup games with Wednesday. Here, in his role as club skipper, he is making a presentation to Joe Shaw, a veteran of 20 major derbies plus many more in County Cup and testimonials. Looking on are Len Allchurch, Mick Jones, Tony Wagstaff and Derek Pace.

Len Badger got his first taste of a 'big time' derby day on the September afternoon in 1964 when his pal Alan Birchenall scored both goals in a 2-0 win for the Blades at Hillsborough. He was involved in making one of the goals in the 200th derby in 1966.

Record for Fantham

WHEN Wednesday and United shared a 1-1 draw at Hillsborough in January 1968, it was to be the last Sheffield derby in the top grade for 23 years, and the occasion also had a place in the records as the game in which Wednesday's Johnny Fantham claimed the Owls' aggregate post-war scoring record.

The 141st League goal of Fantham's career came in the 54th minute, and, while it was hardly a classic strike, it was a finish so typical of the former Burngreave schoolboy's knack of snapping up chances. A Jim McCalliog shot had been stopped by Alan Hodgkinson and Fantham pounced to profit from the rebound.

United equalised after 70 minutes when Mick Hill scored with a fine shot on the run after terrific work by little Willie Carlin.

Wednesday: P.Springett; Smith, Megson, Branfoot, Mobley, Young, Whitham, Symm, Ritchie, McCalliog, Fantham.

United: Hodgkinson; Badger, Shaw, Munks, Mallender, Wagstaff, Woodward, Carlin, Hill, Addison, Reece.

Referee: Jim Finney (Hereford).

When the Sheffield clubs met for the 201st time, at Bramall Lane in February 1967, Wednesday had Peter Wicks making his derby debut, and here he is seen collecting a high cross despite the challenge of Mick Jones. Vic Mobley is defending on the goal-line, while Alan Woodward waits to pounce on any mistake by the goalkeeper.

Bill Punton (11) follows the ball into the net after scoring the goal that won the derby match of February 1967 at Bramall Lane, with Peter Wicks grounded and Wilf Smith helpless.

Alan Woodward, shown in action here later in his United career, scored the first goal in the 200th Sheffield derby game in 1966.

Wednesday's Tommy Craig celebrates his goal for the Owls at Bramall Lane, October 1970.

Above: Scottish winger Jackie Sinclair slots Wednesday's second goal past Alan Hodgkinson, October 1970.

September 1966 Teams:
Wednesday: Springett; Smith, Megson, Eustace, Ellis, Young, Pugh, Fantham, McCalliog, Ford, Quinn.
United: Hodgkinson; Badger, Shaw(Munks, 14 mins), Mallender, Matthewson, Barlow, Woodward, Wagstaff, Jones, Birchenall, Reece.
Referee: A.W.S.Jones (Ormskirk)

1970-71 Derby Days

THE 1970-71 campaign was the one in which the Sheffield clubs met in the old Second Division for the first time since 1959, and it was the

Left, top: Wednesday goalkeeper Peter Grummitt saves at the feet of United's Gil Reece, with Allan Thompson in attendance.

Left, bottom: United goalkeeper Alan Hodgkinson collects the ball with Alan Warboys challenging.

Eddie Colquhoun – the Blades skipper was on target in the 3-2 defeat of the Owls at Bramall Lane.

In the Hillsborough return of April 1970, United's Eddie Colquhoun is seen in an aerial challenge with Wednesday strikers Mick Prendergast and David Sunley. Also in the picture are United's Gil Reece, Frank Barlow and Billy Dearden. Later in his career, Barlow joined the Wednesday staff.

JOHN TUDOR, the striker who came on as substitute and scored the winning goal in the derby duel at Bramall Lane in October 1970, but had left and moved to Newcastle before the return fixture in April. This picture, taken during a match against Huddersfield in August 1969, is of interest in showing the old Pavilion score-board in the background.

Hillsborough derby 1970 – United's John Flynn climbs above Wednesday's Allan Thompson to get in a header. Colin Prophett is the other Owls defender.

Blades, taking three points from the two derby fixtures, who went on to win promotion.

In the first game, watched by 39,983 at Bramall Lane in October, United won 3-2 with goals from Eddie Colquhoun, Billy Dearden and match-winning substitute John Tudor, with Tommy Craig and Jack Sinclair on target for the Owls.

The return fixture, which attracted 47,406 to Hillsborough in April, ended in a 0-0 draw.

Boxing Day Blues for the Blades

Hillsborough, 26 December 1979: Wednesday 4 United 0

A RECORD Third Division crowd of 49,309 packed into Hillsborough for the 100th League and Cup derby between the Sheffield clubs and the first in the Football League outside the top two divisions; and the Boxing Day game of 1979, which kicked off at 11am, earned a special place in local sporting folklore. It was a duel which marked a turning point in the fortunes of the Owls and the Blades.

It was the first League meeting of the Sheffield clubs

Mike Pickering, the Owls' skipper, said: "I never played in an atmosphere quite like that at Hillsborough in the Boxing Day derby of 1979."

Crowd scenes at Hillsborough, Boxing Day 1979.

Wednesday's Brian Hornsby (6) raises his arms in triumph as a 25-yard shot from Ian Mellor (not in picture) gives Wednesday the lead.

since 1971. At the time United were the promotion pacemakers and Wednesday, with two wins in their previous seven matches, were trailing them by six points. But defeat knocked the Blades off their stride while victory set the Owls up for a run which led to a place in the Second Division.

Wednesday captain, Mick Pickering, just back in the side after missing 16 games with a knee injury, described it as the most unforgettable match of a career which spanned over 400 League matches. He said: "I'll never forget the feeling as we walked out from the tunnel and into this terrific wall of noise. I never played in an atmosphere quite like it. It's an experience I'll always treasure, and the only pity was the game passed so quickly."

It was an especially memorable day for Wednesday's 17-year-old left-back, Charlie Williamson, making his home debut and only his second senior appearance. He was given his chance because of a suspension

Ian Mellor is hugged by Mark Smith, and Terry Curran (11) salutes Wednesday's first goal.

David Grant was serving.

It was a fairly even first half-hour, but Wednesday made the breakthrough five minutes before half-time when Ian Mellor scored with a 25-yard effort; and United, having seen home goalkeeper Bob Bolder deny them an equaliser when turning a shot on to the bar, suffered a further blow 12 minutes after the interval when they lost skipper Mick Speight injured. John Cutbush deputised.

Worse followed for the Blades. On 63 minutes Andy McCulloch set up a chance for Terry Curran to head Wednesday's second (earlier Curran and Jeff King had both hit United's post), and, within another couple of minutes, King made it 3-0 after Curran had drawn out goalkeeper Derek Richardson and fed his colleague. Ironically, both King (in 1981) and Curran (1982) subsequently joined United.

The rout was completed three minutes from the end when local lad Mark Smith scored from the penalty-spot

Blades goalkeeper Richardson is beaten by Curran's diving header which made it 2-0 to Wednesday.

Terry Curran (left) is congratulated by Andy McCulloch after heading Wednesday's second goal.

Mark Smith scored Wednesday's fourth from the penalty-spot after Richardson brought down Curran.

Charlie Williamson, seen here signing professional forms under the watchful eye of Owls manager Jack Charlton, made only his second League appearance in the famous Boxing Day derby of 1979.

Goalkeeper Richardson and the Blades defence under pressure from McCulloch.

after Richardson (he was making only his second appearance) brought down Curran. Within minutes of the final whistle, Owls fans were hailing what they will always remember as 'the Boxing Day massacre' – and Blades' followers had a long time to wait for revenge.

In the return game at Bramall Lane the following April the

Blades skipper Mick Speight, who was forced to retire injured 12 minutes after half-time, is seen here explaining the source of his pain to United coach Cec Coldwell and Wednesday trainer Tony Toms.

The duel between Wednesday's Terry Curran and United's Tony Kenworthy was one of the features of the Bramall Lane game. Here Kenworthy stops the Owls' hero with a decisive tackle.

Derby Day at Bramall Lane, April 1980. Owls defender
Mick Pickering heading clear.

*United's Tony Kenworthy grounded and requiring
treatment. Kenworthy's duel with Curran (11) was
one of the features of the game. United's Garner,
MacPhail and Sabella are also in the picture.*

Wednesday's Ian Mellor gets in a header on the Blades' goal in the return game at Bramall Lane, 1980.

teams shared a 1-1 draw in a
duel remembered for a brilliant
equaliser by Terry Curran after
John MacPhail had given the
Blades the lead in what was to

be the last League derby
between the clubs until 1991.
However, they did meet in the
Football League Cup over two
first-round legs in August 1980.

The Boxing Day teams at
Hillsborough were:

Wednesday: Bolder;
Blackhall, Williamson, Smith,
Pickering, Hornsby, King,

The three points the Owls claimed from the derby duels in 1979-80 significantly contributed to their successful promotion push, and The Star marked the triumph with this souvenir picture.

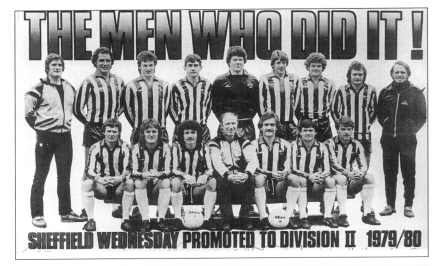

Johnson, McCulloch, Mellor, Curran.

United: Richardson; Speight(Cutbush), Tibbott, Kenworthy, MacPhail, Matthews, de Goey, Bourne, Butlin, Garner, Sabella.

For the record, the line-up on derby day at Bramall Lane in April 1980 was:
United: Poole; Cutbush, Tibbott, Kenworthy(Flood), MacPhail, Jones, de Goey, Speight, Butlin, Sabella, Garner.
Wednesday: Bolder; Blackhall, Grant, Smith, Pickering, Hornsby, Taylor, Johnson, Mellor, Lowey, Curran.

Terry Curran, whose brilliant goal earned the Owls a point, is congratulated by Blades goalkeeper Terry Poole as they leave the field at the end of the Bramall Lane game.

They Served Both Clubs

CARL BRADSHAW joined Wednesday from school in 1985 and made his League debut in 1986, completing 32 League games for the Owls and then having a spell at Manchester City before returning to Sheffield in September 1989 to play with the Blades, the team he supported as a boy. He made over 150 League and Cup appearances for United and figured in some notable triumphs over the Owls before moving to Norwich in 1994.

JOE COCKROFT was a West Ham wing-half when he began with the Owls in wartime football and helped Wednesday reach the League North Cup Final in 1943. He was Wednesday's first post-war skipper, and completed 97 League and Cup outings before his unexpected £4,000 transfer to United in November 1948 when, at the age of 37 years and five months, he became the oldest player to make his First Division debut. Cockroft played only 12 League games for the Blades – and twice missed a penalty! His Owls debut was as a guest against United at Bramall Lane on Christmas Day 1940, and he was in the side that crushed United 8-2 in February 1943.

TERRY CURRAN, seen here signing for United watched by Blades manager Ian Porterfield, was the sometimes brilliant but often temperamental winger who cost the Owls £100,000 from Southampton in early 1979 and helped them win promotion from Division Three in 1980. After 138 games (39 goals) he made a £100,000 move across the city, making 33 League appearances in the red-and-white. Curran scored an outstanding goal for Wednesday in the Third Division derby game at Bramall Lane in April 1980, having earlier figured in the famous Boxing Day triumph at Hillsborough.

TEDDY DAVISON. Between 1908 and 1925 'Honest' Teddy, the smallest goalkeeper to play for England, made over 400 League and Cup appearances for Wednesday; and, from 1932 to 1952, he was Sheffield United's secretary-manager. The famous 'George Washington' tale is in an earlier part of this book.

SIMON STAINROD was a local lad who started his career at Sheffield United, for whom he made 67 League appearances in the 1970s. He later played with Oldham and QPR and in February 1985 cost the Owls a record £260,000 fee, but managed only 15 outings (seven as substitute) before moving to Aston Villa in the following September.

JACK HUDSON, one of Sheffield's England internationals of the Victorian era and a great Wednesday hero in the years before and at the start of the club's professional era in the 1880s. After the birth of the Blades in 1889 he wore the red-and-white of Sheffield United.

NEIL RAMSBOTTOM, the much-travelled goalkeeper who made 18 League appearances for Wednesday in 1975-76 also had two outings for United in 1979.

FRANZ CARR, who played for United in the famous Sheffield derby at Wembley in 1993, had a spell on loan with Wednesday earlier in his career.

DAVID FORD, an England Under-23 forward who played for Wednesday in the 1966 FA Cup Final and served the Owls from 1963 to 1969, moving in at Bramall Lane (where this picture was taken) in January 1971 after a spell at Newcastle. He helped the Blades win promotion that same season. Ford played over 120 League games for Wednesday, 27 for United. It is of interest to note that when he went on as a substitute against Wednesday in Len Badger's testimonial in March 1973 he scored United's equaliser with his first kick after Brian Joicey had headed the Owls in front.

BERT OSWALD was with the Blades from 1930 to 1934. After moving to Wednesday he did not manage a game in the League side.

JEFF KING joined Wednesday from Walsall in August 1979 and made 68 appearances before moving across the city in January 1982 and managing 37 League outings with the Blades. King was in the Owls team that beat United 4-0 on Boxing Day 1979, and scored a goal.

WILF ROSTRON was a former Watford, Arsenal and Sunderland player who made seven League appearances for Wednesday in 1989 and later the same year played in the first of 36 League games for United.

BERNARD SHAW, brother of Graham Shaw (the man who made his Blades debut in the Sheffield derby of January 1952). Full-back Bernard made 136 League appearances for United after his 1963 debut, and arrived at Hillsborough from Wolves in 1973. He had 113 outings for the Owls.

WALTER RICKETT, (left), the little winger with a big heart, has a special place in Sheffield derby history, for, when he made his first appearance in a United-Wednesday match, at Bramall Lane in March 1940, he scored for the Blades with his very first kick in a 4-3 victory! It was the first of five goals Walter scored against the Owls in the war years. Rickett had 57 League outings for United after the war before moving to Blackpool, but he returned to Sheffield in October 1949 and made 97 appearances for the Owls. One of his Wednesday games was on the day in September 1952 when United beat the Owls 7-3 at Bramall Lane!

IMRE VARADI made only ten League appearances for the Blades (four of them as a substitute) before being sold to Everton for a substantial fee in March 1979. He returned to Sheffield in 1983 when he joined the Owls from Newcastle. In two spells with Wednesday Varadi scored 36 goals in 98 League games.

GEORGE UNDERWOOD was a local lad who made 17 League appearances for United and was transferred to Wednesday in October 1951. He never played in the Owls' League side and moved on to Scunthorpe in 1953. He played for Wednesday reserves in the Central League derby at Bramall Lane on that famous occasion in September 1952 when Dooley, dropped from the Owls' senior team, ended his goal-famine with two strikes against the Blades in the last five minutes.

GEORGE WALLER, a Pitsmoor product who played for Wednesday in the 1890 FA Cup final but later joined United, with whom he soon gave up playing to concentrate on the role in which he became a Bramall Lane legend – trainer to the first team over a span of some 40 years until his retirement in the 1930s.

DEREK DOOLEY, *the great Wednesday scoring hero of the early post-war era who later managed the Owls and subsequently (in 1974) joined United, where he became a director and ultimately managing director. By 1995 he boasted a unique place in Sheffield football history with a 48-year link with professional soccer in the city.*

BILLY MOSFORTH was one of Sheffield football's legendary figures, the darling of local fans in the Victorian era. He played with Wednesday from around 1877 to 1889 and, like teammate Jack Hudson, offered his services to the newly-formed Sheffield United.

FRANK BARLOW. As a product of Sheffield United's 1960s youth policy, he was one of the club's many Don & Dearne 'discoveries' and made 121 League appearances at wing-half in the Blades' colours. It was in Peter Eustace's brief spell as Wednesday's manager in the late 1980s that Frank joined the Owls' training staff, and he subsequently filled a key role in charge of Wednesday's reserves.

ALAN WARBOYS played for the Owls from 1968 to 1970 after being signed from Doncaster, he scored 13 goals in 82 games before being sold to Cardiff. He returned to Sheffield in 1972 to play for United, but managed only seven League outings in a brief and disappointing spell.

IAN PORTERFIELD played in some 130 games for Wednesday between 1977 and 1980, and, in 1981, after a successful if brief spell as team boss at Rotherham, he became Sheffield United's manager and remained at Bramall Lane until March 1986. Twice he led the Blades to promotion.

JOHN HARRIS, the Scot whose name was synonymous with Sheffield United from March 1959 until the mid-1970s. He was a manager with a happy knack of making bargain signings who became Bramall Lane heroes – with Len Allchurch, Gil Reece, Tony Currie and Billy Dearden among his finest buys. When the Blades decided 'Gentleman' John was surplus to requirements, he was snapped up by Wednesday when Len Ashurst appointed him chief scout. Harris was later assistant to Jack Charlton. He was forced to retire owing to ill-health and died in July 1988 at the age of 71.

GEORGE McCABE, best known as a Football League referee, he was a goalkeeper with Wednesday in the war years. Later he was a member of the Owls' back room staff, and he subsequently had a role at Bramall Lane. He was 'the man in the middle' on the famous occasion in October 1955 when Wednesday and United met in a 'secret' derby duel behind closed doors at Hillsborough.

FRANK MELLING. *A dashing amateur centre-forward who scored 35 goals in 55 games for Wednesday from 1941 to 1943 and helped them reach the League North War Cup Final. In 1943 he scored two goals in the 8-2 defeat of United and hit the winner in a 3-2 success against the Blades. Ironically, the man who later earned fame as a Sheffield United cricket captain joined the Bramall Lane club's board in 1954 and spent some 25 years as a director.*

BERNARD OXLEY *played with United from 1928 to 1934, when he moved to Wednesday. He scored for United in the 3-1 defeat of the Owls in January 1931. He spent barely a year at Hillsborough before moving to Plymouth.*

GEORGE COLE. *A centre-half who never played in Wednesday's League team, he was snapped up on a free transfer by United in 1937. He made only one League appearance for the Blades, in their 5-3 win at Swansea in November 1937.*

Men who have been on the books of one Sheffield club and guested with the other in wartime matches include: Harold Barton, C.Brelsford, Tom Cawley jun, Douglas Hunt, Tom Johnson, Walter Millership, Jack Smith, Hugh Swift, Oliver Tummon, Fred White.

BRIAN MARWOOD made 128 League appearances for Wednesday between August 1984 and March 1988, and arrived at Bramall Lane in September 1990 after a spell with Arsenal, but managed only 22 League outings for the Blades.

Here's a novelty picture for the derby day records – the occasion in 1990 when Blades' legend Tony Currie donned an Owls shirt and played for Wednesday in a testimonial fixture.

Zenith Data Systems Cup 1989

21 November 1989: Wednesday 3 United 2 (after extra-time)

THE first meeting of the Sheffield clubs in a Cup fixture since 1980 created tremendous interest and, although the ZDS (formerly Full Members') Cup was hardly expected to capture the public imagination like the FA Cup and the League Cup, this floodlit second-round tie attracted a staggering 30,464 to Hillsborough – a record for the competition.

The match winner, with a marvellous solo run and strike in the third minute of extra-time, was Wednesday's Republic of Ireland midfielder John Sheridan, whose goal provided a classic finish to an absorbing duel often described as a contrast in styles and an occasion to remember – all the more so as it confirmed that the passion for football remained as strong as ever in Sheffield.

Dalian Atkinson gave Wednesday the lead after 19 minutes with a superb shot on the run, but Brian Deane levelled for United after 34 minutes. Carlton Palmer thought he had snatched victory for the Owls with four minutes remaining, but Bob Booker took the game into extra-time when he equalised after 89 minutes.

Wednesday: Pressman; Pearson, Shirtliff, Madden, King, Palmer, Bennett(Shakespeare 105 mins), Sheridan, Hirst, Atkinson, Worthington.

United: Tracey; Hill, Barnes, Booker, Stancliffe, Morris, Bradshaw(Francis 75 mins), Gannon, Agana(Webster 81 mins), Deane, Bryson.

Match programme cover

Dalian Atkinson (right) fires the Owls in front in the ZDS tie.

Brian Deane equalises, pouncing on the loose ball when Pressman failed to hold a Bryson shot

United's Tony Agana under challenge from Wednesday's Peter Shirtliff.

Blades' skipper Paul Stancliffe celebrates Deane's goal.

Sheridan strikes magical winner

– "Sheridan Strikes Magical Winner". As Chris Wilson of The Yorkshire Post saw it on the night.

Sheffield W 3 Sheffield U 2   By CHRIS WILSON

A BRILLIANT goal in the third minute of extra time by John Sheridan tipped the Sheffield derby Wednesday's way after an incredible Cup tie at

evening, launched into an amazing run down the left flank, reaching the edge of the United penalty area before the back pedalling defence even thought

memorable occasion. The match was fiercely competitive without becoming dirty while the crowd of 3?,464 played their part in up a head

Wednesday had gone in front after 19 minutes when Atkinson latched on to a long pass by Madden, turned inside United's centre backs and fired a superb shot on the run into the roof of the net. United had gone se to with

Carlton Palmer salutes the Hillsborough Kop after his 86th minute goal in the ZDS match.

Sweet Sheri! Wednesday's John Sheridan completes a memorable run with a tremendous strike which sealed a famous Zenith Data Systems Cup victory over the Blades.

John Sheridan, celebrating his winning goal, with Dalian Atkinson and Nigel Worthington.

1991-92: Together Again in Division One

Sunday, 17 November 1991: United 2 Wednesday 0

Wednesday, 11 March 1992: Wednesday 1 United 3

THE 1991-92 campaign is remembered as the one in which the Sheffield clubs met in the top grade for the first time since 1968 – and the Blades romped to their first double over the Owls for 30 years with memorable triumphs which defied the form

Cover of United-Wednesday match programme, 17 November 1991.

book at Bramall Lane and Hillsborough. The eagerly-awaited first meeting, watched by a 31,803 crowd at the Lane in November, kicked off at noon and proved something of a culture shock for Wednesday. With United propping up the First Division, everybody except Blades supporters seemed to think victory would be a formality for Trevor Francis' men. However, on the day, Dave Bassett's boys had all the passion and quite literally caught their city rivals cold.

United's Tom Cowan and Wednesday's Danny Wilson in a heading duel during the first Sheffield derby in the top grade for 23 years, at Bramall Lane in November 1991.

Wednesday did get the ball in the net at Bramall Lane but this Viv Anderson effort was nullified by an offside decision.

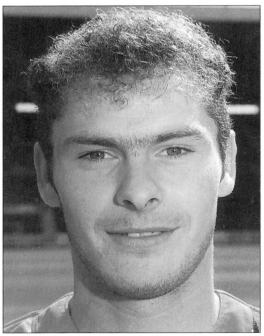

Dane Whitehouse, a Sheffield product who had seen his first derby as a small boy when he was taken to witness the Boxing Day game of 1979, he long dreamed of helping United avenge that painful defeat; and, happily, he scored the first goal in each of the 1991-92 derbies to contribute to a memorable Blades double.

The opening goal, just before half-time, came courtesy of a collision between Wednesday men John Sheridan and Paul Warhurst which allowed Ian Bryson to pick up the loose ball and race away; and although Chris Woods in the Owls' goal knocked the Scot's shot aside, Dane Whitehouse pounced to score from the rebound – a thrilling moment for a local boy whose first sight of a Sheffield derby had been when he was taken to the famous 1979 Boxing Day duel at Hillsborough.

Wednesday won 12 corners to United's five, but Simon Tracey was in good form in the home goal, and the Blades completed a deserved success when Brian Deane made it 2-0 after 72 minutes with a shot which went through the legs of Woods.

Jamie Hoyland was following in his father's footsteps, for Tom had played in three League derbies for United in the 1950s and finished on the winning side each time.

The teams were:

United: Tracey; Pemberton, Gayle, Beesley, Cowan, Gannon, Bradshaw, Hoyland, Whitehouse, Bryson, Deane.

Wednesday: Woods; Nilsson, Warhurst, Anderson, King, Palmer, Wilson(Harkes 73 mins), Sheridan, Worthington, Hirst, P.Williams.

The return game at

Jamie Hoyland emulated his father, Tom in helping the Blades triumph over Wednesday when he figured in Sheffield's first top-grade derby since 1968.

Carl Bradshaw, once of Wednesday but always a Blades fan as a boy, in the double triumph of 1991-92 he epitomised the passion and determination of a United side which many had rated unlikely to seriously test the 'cultured' Owls. It was Bradshaw's long ball into the home goalmouth at Hillsborough which set up United's first goal.

rainswept Hillsborough in March is remembered as the night Derek Dooley saw Wednesday play a home game for the first time since his days as the Owls' team manager. He was given a tremendous welcome by home fans – but now, as a 'true Blade', he was delighted to see the Lane lads register another famous victory in front of a 40,327 crowd.

Wednesday, without Nigel Worthington, experimented with three centre-backs, but it was silly defensive slips rather than tactical failings that pushed

them to defeat. In truth, they played better than they had in November, but United's finishing paid a deserved dividend.

Whitehouse shot United in front after only four minutes, and they were two up on 28 minutes when ex-Owl Carl Bradshaw's long ball into the goalmouth rebounded-off Woods and Bobby Davison, making his first appearance on loan from Leeds, hooked the rebound into the net.

Wednesday reduced arrears after 49 minutes when Phil King, collecting the ball from

Danny Wilson's free-kick, hammered his first goal in 125 matches for the club. But that man Davison made it 3-1 with a diving header when John Gannon drove in a sharp cross from the right.

Wednesday: Woods; Anderson, Shirtliff, Pearson(Harkes 72 mins); Nilsson, Wilson(Jemson 69 mins), Hyde, Palmer, King; Hirst, P.Williams.

United: Tracey; Gage, Gayle, Beesley, Barnes; Bradshaw, Gannon, Rogers, Whitehouse(Hodges 64 mins); Davison(Cork 80 mins), Deane.

United's two-goal hero Bobby Davison (right) in a confrontation with Wednesday's Danny Wilson

Davison delivers United double

By Keith Farnsworth

Sheffield Wednesday 1   Sheffield Utd 3

SHEFFIELD UNITED com-
pleted their first double over
neighbours Wednesday since
1962 as a Bobby Davison
debut double and a goal from
local boy Dane Whitehouse
...

his loan move from Leeds.
United were close again after
40 minutes, when Davison's
left-wing cross eluded the
unmarked Deane at the far
post with Woods beaten.
...

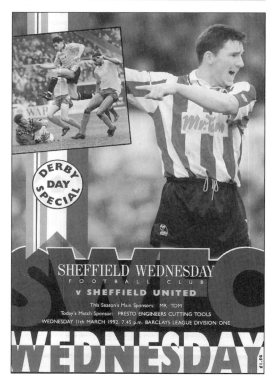

Derby rivals: United's Brian Deane and Wednesday's Viv Anderson.

Derby Day match programme: Wednesday v United, March 1992.

1992-93: The First Premiership Derbies

Sunday, 8 November 1992: United 1 Wednesday 1

Wednesday, 21 April 1993: Wednesday 1 United 1

IN THE game at Bramall Lane in November, the first half was fairly even, with United's Alan Kelly denying Mark Bright with one fine save and Wednesday's Woods frustrating Adrian Littlejohn with another – while Blades' striker Brian Deane also hit the bar.

United took the lead after

An aerial duel between Wednesday's Mark Bright and United's Paul Beesley in the 1992 Bramall Lane duel.

The rival managers, United's Dave Bassett (left) and Wednesday's Trevor Francis.

Tempers flare in a goalmouth incident in the Hillsborough derby of April 1993.

61 minutes when Mitch Ward's corner drew Woods from his goal, and, when Deane headed the ball goalwards, Littlejohn somehow got the faintest of touches with the back of his heel to guide it into the net despite the efforts of Danny Wilson standing on the goal-line.

Glyn Hodges, United's Welsh international, was sent off ten minutes before the end of the Hillsborough game for an off-the-ball incident involving Wednesday's United States international John Harkes.

Six minutes later, Wednesday made a tactical switch, replacing John Sheridan with Paul Warhurst, and it paid off. However, it was not until the 84th minute that the Owls equalised through David Hirst. A one-two with Chris Waddle saw the striker collect a perfectly weighted return pass and, with typical economy of effort, score a memorable goal.

The teams were:

United: Kelly; Gage, Gayle, Beesley, Cowan, Bradshaw,

A memorable goal from Wednesday's David Hirst as he ends a one-two with Chris Waddle and delivers a classic strike which gives United goalkeeper Alan Kelly no chance while earning the Owls a 1-1 draw at Bramall Lane.

Ward(Hodges 86 mins), Rogers, Gannon, Littlejohn, Deane. Unused subs: Hoyland, Kite (goalkeeper).

Wednesday: Woods; Nilsson, Pearson, Palmer, Worthington, Waddle, Wilson, Sheridan(Warhurst 67 mins), Bart-Williams, Hirst, Bright. Unused subs: Harkes, Pressman (goalkeeper)

The Hillsborough return in April, of course, came after the famous Wembley derby. It also followed Wednesday's defeat in the Coca-Cola Cup Final, and injury problems meant Paul Warhurst starting the game in defence. To add to their problems, Ryan Jones was carried off after seven minutes following a knock suffered when he threw himself into the goalmouth for a diving header;

and, late in a tough duel, Chris Waddle had to retire following a hard challenge by Charlie Hartfield

United opened the scoring against the run of play a minute before half-time, when Woods was beaten by Deane, who profited from a Glyn Hodges centre from the left. The Owls pulled level after 78 minutes when the decision to switch Warhurst into attack paid a prompt dividend. John Harkes swung the ball into the goalmouth, Hirst glanced it on, and Warhurst scored with a shot which went in off a post.

Two minutes later the Blades had Glyn Hodges sent off by referee Ken Redfearn for an off-the-ball incident in which it was alleged he elbowed Harkes. It was a physical battle at times, though United

manager Dave Bassett commented: "One or two players were having a little push during the game, but most of it was handbags stuff. However, we didn't need to go down to ten men just when they'd equalised."

Teams:

Wednesday: Woods; Nilsson, Palmer, Warhurst, Worthington, Waddle(Bart-Williams 77 mins), Sheridan, Jones(Hyde 7 mins), Harkes, Hirst, Bright. Unused sub: Pressman (goalkeeper).

United: Kelly; Ward, Gayle, Pemberton, Beesley, Bradshaw, Hartfield, Rogers, Hodges, Deane(Scott 89 mins), Whitehouse. Unused subs: Hoyland, Leighton (goalkeeper).

A Sheffield Derby at Wembley!

FA Cup semi-final, Saturday, 3 April 1993

Wednesday 2 United 1 (after extra-time)

A 75,364 crowd packed into Wembley for the most memorable Sheffield derby of them all – the unique FA Cup semi-final of April 1993. A happy and colourful affair played in a carnival atmosphere: the Steel City's own Cup Final produced one of those days when supporters of the two clubs set a wonderful example to the nation of how to enjoy a football match in a spirit of mutual goodwill.

When the Blades and the Owls both progressed to the last four in the same season for the first time in FA Cup history

The whole of Sheffield celebrated the appearance of the city's premier teams in the unique FA Cup semi-final at Wembley, and here the children of Greenhill Primary School, supporters of both the Blades and the Owls, prepare for an end-of-term concert with a football flavour.

and were paired in the draw, the Football Association wanted the match to be staged at Elland Road, Leeds. But Sheffield fans knew there was only one venue fit for this very special event – Wembley Stadium. And, thankfully, the authorities listened to the arguments and, albeit reluctantly, finally agreed.

It ensured a day the

Wembley rivals but friends just the same: managers Dave Bassett (United) and Trevor Francis (Wednesday) smile before the action begins.

Sheffield brings a carnival atmosphere to Wembley as thousands of balloons are released before the game.

Waddle's stunning free-kick screeches into the net leaving the diving Kelly helpless.

Chris Waddle leading United men Whitehouse and Gannon a dance on the famous Wembley turf.

Christ Waddle – man of the match at Wembley and Footballer of the Year in 1993, the Wednesday favourite produced a sensational start to the semi-final derby when he hammered a 28-yard free-kick past United's Alan Kelly barely a minute after the kick-off.

Wednesday well deserved a triumph clinched in extra-time. Beyond the match itself there were no losers from Sheffield: it was a derby which might never be matched, and it will remain a source of pride for many years to be able to say 'I was there'.

The first outstanding memory of the game was an superb early strike by Wednesday's Chris Waddle, who beat United goalkeeper Alan Kelly with a stunning 28-yard free-kick less than 65 seconds after the kick-off following John Pemberton's nudge on Mark Bright.

Other memories included Paul Warhurst hitting the Blades bar, and some brilliant saves by Kelly from substitute David Hirst, John Sheridan and Mark Bright. Republic of Ireland goalkeeper Kelly was the top rival to Waddle for the man-of-the-match award.

Then there was Alan Cork's equaliser almost on half-time when Franz Carr (who had once had a spell on loan with Wednesday) set up the chance and the balding and bearded United striker, unshaven through the Cup run, found the net despite the valiant efforts of Waddle as he ran back towards his own goal and made a desperate bid to prevent the ball crossing the line.

In truth, Wednesday dominated but took a long time to get the pay-off, and there were times when it was not beyond the realms of possibility that United would snatch victory against all the odds – perhaps to avenge that undeserved defeat of 1960.

But, after 107 minutes, the winning goal finally arrived. John Harkes won a corner on

travelling multitudes of Sheffield football fans will never forget, and such was their behaviour and the quality of the match that the city won millions of new friends and admirers, and the FA had to admit the teams and followers of United and Wednesday

brought nothing but credit to English football.

The only disappointment was someone had to lose in a duel which spanned 120 minutes. In the event, it was United who went down – but with their heads held high and conceding that, on the day,

Paul Warhurst, the Owls' defender-turned-striker, gets in a shot despite the attentions of Blades' skipper Brian Gayle.

*Battling for the ball...
Wednesday's Carlton Palmer and
United's Alan Cork.*

the left, and the US international lifted the ball into the goalmouth, where Bright, escaping the attentions of Brian Deane, rose to head past Kelly. Owls boss Trevor Francis had told Bright before the game that he would be the match-winner, and the prediction came true. A final memory at the end was watching the Wednesday manager run up the steps to the royal box to

Striker Alan Cork is hugged by Franz Carr after scoring United's equaliser just before half-time.

Wednesday's Harkes and United's Carr in a touch-line duel at Wembley.

Wednesday substitute David Hirst (right) and United defender John Pemberton dispute possession, with Blades' skipper Brian Gayle looking on.

The Wembley winner. Mark Bright beats Brian Deane to the John Harkes corner and finally get the better of United goalkeeper Alan Kelly as his header seals extra-time success for the Owls.

Worthington, Sheridan and Harkes, just three of Wednesday's heroes at Wembley.

Brian Deane, the Blades' striker, is beaten to the ball by Wednesday's Carlton Palmer.

greet his wife Helen and his sons Matthew and James.

Alas, Wednesday lost in the FA Cup Final, in a replay, having earlier fallen in the Coca-Cola Cup Final, and, with the benefit of hindsight, it was not difficult to see that the Wembley triumph over Manchester United was the high point of the Francis era. By mid-1995 he would have left Hillsborough.

United	Wednesday
Alan Kelly	Chris Woods
Kevin Gage	Roland Nilsson
Brian Gayle	Carlton Palmer
John Pemberton	Viv Anderson
Dane Whitehouse	Nigel Worthington
Franz Carr	Chris Waddle
John Gannon	Danny Wilson
Mitch Ward	John Sheridan
Glyn Hodges	John Harkes
Brian Deane	Paul Warhurst
Alan Cork	Mark Bright
Subs: Adrian Littlejohn (96 mins)for Ward, Jamie Hoyland (91 mins) for Hodges.	David Hirst (60 mins) for Warhurst. Graham Hyde (110 mins) for Sheridan.
Referee: K.Morton (Suffolk)	

Owls' manager Trevor Francis and match-winner Mark Bright celebrate Wednesday's Wembley triumph. "I told Mark before the game that he would score the winning goal," said Francis.

Premiership 1993-94

Saturday, 23 October 1993: United 1 Wednesday 1

Saturday, 22 January 1994: Wednesday 3 United 1

NEITHER side was doing very well at the time of 97th League derby in October 1993, for United were without a win in eight Premiership matches and Wednesday had won one in 12. Moreover, since beating the Blades at Wembley the previous season, the Owls had won only four of 24 matches.

So, perhaps it was no surprise when the duel at Bramall Lane (where Wednesday had won only two League games in 60 years) ended in a 1-1 draw. United manager Dave Bassett summed it up as 'a non-event'.

Glyn Hodges gave United the lead after seven minutes, pouncing to lob into the net

Blades' Joy! Mitch Ward and Glyn Hodges celebrate the Welsh international's early goal at Bramall Lane in October 1993.

High ball for Wednesday goalkeeper Kevin Pressman to deal with as the Blades attack.

A 'foreign' note on derby day at Bramall Lane as Wednesday's Swedish defender Roland Nilsson and United's Norwegian forward Jostein Flo chase a ball, with Owls' Australian Adem Poric looking on.

Aerial attack – Flo beats Wednesday's Des Walker to a high cross.

after Owls goalkeeper Kevin Pressman had pushed out Mitch Ward's cross. However, Wednesday were level within five minutes after Mark Bright got away on the left and Carlton Palmer timed his dash into the goalmouth perfectly, meeting his colleague's cross from the left with a fine header which gave Simon Tracey no chance.

Teams:

United: Tracey; Bradshaw, Tuttle, Hoyland, Hartfield, Ward(Davison 86 mins), Rogers, Falconer, Hodges, Flo, Cork(Whitehouse 77 mins).

Wednesday: Pressman; Nilsson, Walker, Pearce, Sinton, Poric, Palmer, Hyde, Jones, Waddle, Bright(Jemson 79 mins).

Between the first and second derby games of 1993-94, Wednesday suffered only two defeats in 20 games while United had managed just two wins in 15. On the day the 98th

Wednesday's Palmer and United's Flo obviously don't exactly agree about what constitutes a fair challenge.

League derby went according to the form book. United competed on equal terms for an hour but then succumbed to three strikes in 13 minutes.

The breakthrough came on 58 minutes when Des Walker, Andy Sinton, Palmer and Gordon Watson were involved in the move which led to United goalkeeper Alan Kelly parrying Roland Nilsson's fierce shot and Bright scoring from the rebound.

Within three minutes Andy Pearce had headed in a Sinton cross; and, in the 71st minute, Watson produced a splendid piece of finishing as he nudged the ball past Kelly as the

Wednesday's Andy Sinton and Blades' veteran Alan Cork put maximum effort into a midfield duel.

Orders from the Blades' bench – manager Dave Bassett, anxious to maintain his unbeaten record against the Owls, shouts instructions from the touch-line. Assistant manager Geoff Taylor and physio Derek French are among those looking on, plus Wally Downes, who sports unusual headgear.

Tracey's ball! The Blades' goalkeeper beats Ryan Jones to a high cross in the 1-1 draw at Bramall Lane.

goalkeeper left his goal, and then squeezed a header just inside the near post.

United's only consolation was an 88th-minute penalty converted by Dane Whitehouse. It was only Wednesday's third win in 16 League derbies since 1965 and the first since 1979; and, as manager Francis said, it was some consolation for earlier disappointments in the series!

Teams:

Wednesday: Pressman; Nilsson, Pearce, Walker, Coleman, Palmer, Hyde, Jones, Sinton(Bart-Williams 85 mins), Bright, Watson.

United: Kelly; Bradshaw, Tuttle, Hoyland(Nilsen 86 mins), Beesley, Ward, Kamara, Hodges, Whitehouse, Flo, Scott.

Referee: K.Cooper (Pontypridd).

Goalmouth action – Blades goalkeeper Alan Kelly just eludes the challenge of Gordon Watson, with Blades defender Jamie Hoyland close at hand in the Hillsborough derby of January 1994.

Making the point… .Blades defender Carl Bradshaw has strong words for Wednesday's Carlton Palmer (4), and gets support from Glyn Hodges, while Owls' goalkeeper Kevin Pressman tries to act as peacemaker, and Dane Whitehouse (left) watches with interest.

Making the point.. It's Carlton Palmer's turn to rebuke Dane Whitehouse, with Mitch Ward and Carl Bradshaw looking on. A case of three Sheffield lads and a recruit from the Midlands!

Jostein Flo gets shirty with Wednesday's Des Walker.

With the Blades relegated from the Premiership at the end of the season, it meant Sheffield football fans faced a delay in witnessing League derbies numbers 99 and 100.

We hope the wait is not too long… and trust the next major derby days will be in the top grade, where the keenness of the quest for points adds that extra edge to the traditional rivalry between the Owls and the Blades!

Shoulder to shoulder – Andy Sinton and Paul Beesley.

Wednesday's second goal in the 3-1 victory at Hillsborough in Sheffield's 98th League derby, with Andy Pearce climbing high to head an Andy Sinton cross past Alan Kelly. Looking on are Carl Bradshaw, Paul Beesley, Gordon Watson, Simon Coleman, Roland Nilsson and David Tuttle.

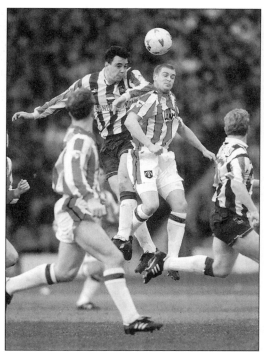

Sheffield-born Mitch Ward gets in a header on the Wednesday goal.

Left: High challenge between Ryan Jones (Wednesday) and Bradshaw (United).

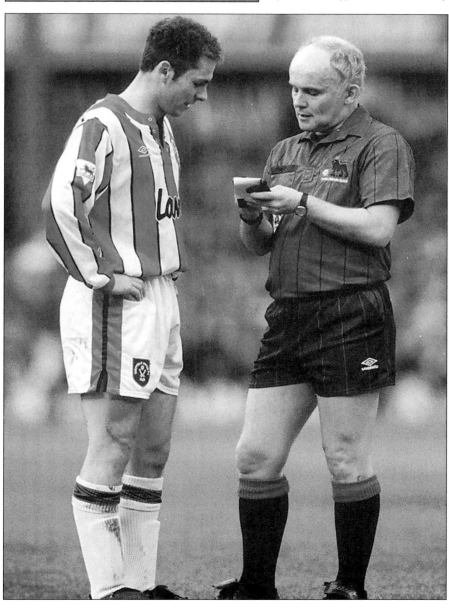

Referee Keith Cooper shows he is the boss when he 'books' Dane Whitehouse.

Sheffield's Football Derbies 1893-1915

#	Date			Venue	Wed	Utd		#	Date			Venue	Wed	Utd
01.	Oct	16	1893	Bramall Lane	1	1		22.	Apr	8	1905	Bramall Lane	2	4
02.	Nov	13	1893	Olive Grove	1	2		23.	Oct	21	1905	Bramall Lane	2	0
03.	Oct	27	1894	Olive Grove	2	3		24.	Apr	18	1906	Owlerton	1	0
04.	Jan	12	1895	Bramall Lane	0	1		25.	Nov	3	1906	Owlerton	2	2
05.	Sep	7	1895	Olive Grove	1	0		26.	Apr	4	1907	Bramall Lane	1	2
06.	Dec	26	1895	Bramall Lane	1	1		27.	Nov	9	1907	Bramall Lane	3	1
07.	Dec	26	1896	Bramall Lane	0	2		28.	Mar	7	1908	Owlerton	2	0
08.	Mar	2	1897	Olive Grove	1	1		29.	Dec	25	1908	Owlerton	1	0
09.	Oct	16	1897	Olive Grove	0	1		30.	Dec	26	1908	Bramall Lane	1	2
10.	Dec	27	1897	Bramall Lane	1	1		31.	Nov	6	1909	Bramall Lane	3	3
11.	Oct	3	1898	Olive Grove	1	1		32.	Mar	19	1910	Owlerton	1	3
12.	Dec	26	1898	Bramall Lane	1	2		33.	Oct	22	1910	Owlerton	2	0
13.	Dec	15	1900	Bramall Lane	0	1		34.	Feb	25	1911	Bramall Lane	1	0
14.	Apr	29	1901	Owlerton	1	0		35.	Nov	4	1911	Bramall Lane	1	1
15.	Nov	2	1901	Owlerton	1	0		36.	Mar	9	1912	Hillsborough	1	1
16.	Mar	1	1902	Bramall Lane	0	3		37.	Oct	26	1912	Hillsborough	1	0
17.	Sep	1	1902	Bramall Lane	3	2		38.	Mar	1	1913	Bramall Lane	2	0
18.	Oct	11	1902	Owlerton	0	1		39.	Oct	25	1913	Bramall Lane	1	0
19.	Dec	12	1903	Bramall Lane	1	1		40.	Feb	28	1914	Hillsborough	2	1
20.	Apr	9	1904	Owlerton	3	0		41.	Sep	5	1914	Bramall Lane	1	0
21.	Dec	10	1904	Owlerton	1	3		42.	Jan	2	1915	Hillsborough	1	1

Sheffield derby 'veterans', Blades' goalkeeper Alan Hodgkinson (left) and Wednesday skipper Don Megson shake hands before the United man's testimonial game in 1968. The referee is George McCabe, who officiated at the 'secret' derby in the mid-1950s.

The Shaw brothers, Bernard (left) and Graham, who both began their careers at Bramall Lane. Bernard later played for Wednesday.

Wednesday skipper Nigel Pearson (left) and United's Tony Agana in action in the Centenary match at Bramall Lane in August 1989.

Joy for Wednesday's Jeff Johnson after scoring against the Blades in the League Cup game at Hillsborough in August 1980. The disconsolate United man is Martin Peters.

Below: Wednesday's Paul Williams (left) scoring against the Blades in the Lawrie Madden testimonial match at Hillsborough, August 1990.

Johnny Fantham, who claimed Wednesday's post-war aggregate scoring record with a goal against the Blades in 1968, was later supported by players from both Sheffield clubs (and they accorded him a guard of honour) when he held his testimonial match in 1970.

Alan Woodward, whose scoring feats brought him United's aggregate post-war goal record, staged a Blades v Owls match when he had his testimonial in 1974.

When United's long-serving player, coach and acting-manager Cec Coldwell (centre) held his testimonial in 1983 he was supported by two men with Wednesday links, Howard Wilkinson and Ian Porterfield. Wilkinson, who had just become manager at Hillsborough, was once an amateur at Bramall Lane. Porterfield, of course, played for Wednesday and managed United.

Some old Blades on duty in a Sheffield Centenary match with veteran Owls at Hillsborough, 1993. Back row (left to right): Tony Currie, Paul Stancliffe, Derek French, Dick Parker, John Dungworth, John Greaves (kitman), Tony Moore, Glyn Hambling. Front row: David Gribben (mascot), Paul Garner, Jim Brown, Chico Hamilton, Len Badger, Ted Hemsley.

More old United favourites return to Bramall Lane for Colin Morris' testimonial and a date with some old Owls in September 1988.

Sheffield's Football League Derbies 1919-1939

					Wed	Utd							Wed	Utd
43.	Sep	27	1919	Hillsborough	2	1	54.	Jan	3	1931	Hillsborough		1	3
44.	Oct	4	1919	Bramall Lane	0	3	55.	Nov	21	1931	Hillsborough		2	1
45.	Aug	28	1926	Hillsborough	2	3	56.	Apr	2	1932	Bramall Lane		1	1
46.	Jan	15	1927	Bramall Lane	0	2	57.	Sep	24	1932	Hillsborough		3	3
47.	Sep	24	1927	Bramall Lane	1	1	58.	Feb	4	1933	Bramall Lane		3	2
48.	Feb	4	1928	Hillsborough	3	3	59.	Oct	21	1933	Hillsborough		0	1
49.	Sep	22	1928	Hillsborough	5	2	60.	Mar	3	1934	Bramall Lane		1	5
50.	Feb	2	1929	Bramall Lane	1	1	61.	Oct	16	1937	Hillsborough		0	1
51.	Sep	28	1929	Bramall Lane	2	2	62.	Feb	26	1938	Bramall Lane		1	2
52.	Feb	1	1930	Hillsborough	1	1	63.	Oct	29	1938	Bramall Lane		0	0
53.	Sep	6	1930	Bramall Lane	1	1	64.	Mar	4	1939	Hillsborough		1	0

Veteran Sheffield football writers, The Star's own Tony Pritchett (left) and freelance Keith Farnsworth, who have seen a few derby matches in their time, welcome the opportunity to discuss derby day opinions with Blades manager Dave Bassett.

One of Harry Heap's traditional Friday evening cartoons from the late 1950s previews a Sheffield derby weekend.

A reunion of Bramall Lane veterans in 1990: (left to right) Tommy Hoyland, Jimmy Hagan, Alf Ringstead and Joe Shaw.

Sheffield United in 1957-58. Back row (left to right): Tommy Hoyland, Alan Hodgkinson, Des Thompson, Joe Shaw. Middle row: Cliff Mason, Gerry Summers, Brian Richardson, Cec Coldwell, Jim Smith, Jim Iley. Front row: Sammy Kemp, Alf Ringstead, Jimmy Hagan, Bobby Howitt, Glyn Jones, Derek Hawksworth.

Sheffield's Post-war Football League Derbies

					Wed	Utd						Wed	Utd
65.	Sep	17	1949	Hillsborough	2	1	80.	Jan	18	1964	Hillsborough	3	0
66.	Jan	21	1950	Bramall Lane	0	2	81.	Sep	5	1964	Hillsborough	0	2
67.	Sep	8	1951	Bramall Lane	3	7	82.	Jan	2	1965	Bramall Lane	3	2
68.	Jan	5	1952	Hillsborough	1	3	83.	Sep	18	1965	Bramall Lane	0	1
69.	Sep	12	1953	Bramall Lane	0	2	84.	Mar	12	1966	Hillsborough	2	2
70.	Jan	23	1954	Hillsborough	3	2	85.	Sep	24	1966	Hillsborough	2	2
71.	Sep	18	1954	Bramall Lane	0	1	86.	Feb	4	1967	Bramall Lane	0	1
72.	Feb	5	1955	Hillsborough	1	2	87.	Sep	7	1967	Bramall Lane	1	0
73.	Oct	4	1958	Hillsborough	2	0	88.	Jan	6	1968	Hillsborough	1	1
74.	Feb	21	1959	Bramall Lane	0	1	89.	Oct	3	1970	Bramall Lane	2	3
75.	Sep	16	1961	Bramall Lane	0	1	90.	Apr	12	1971	Hillsborough	0	0
76.	Feb	3	1962	Hillsborough	1	2	91.	Dec	26	1979	Hillsborough	4	0
77.	Oct	6	1962	Bramall Lane	2	2	92.	Apr	5	1980	Bramall Lane	1	1
78.	May	15	1963	Hillsborough	3	1	93.	Nov	17	1991	Bramall Lane	0	2
79.	Sep	14	1963	Bramall Lane	1	1	94.	Mar	11	1992	Hillsborough	1	3

Sheffield Wednesday 1959-60. Back row (left to right): Tommy Eggleston (coach), Derek Wilkinson, Don Megson, Peter Swan, Ron Springett, Tony Kay, Peter Johnson, Tom McAnearney. Front row: Alan Finney, Keith Ellis, Harry Catterick (manager), Bobby Craig, Johnny Fantham.

Ernest Jackson(left) and Jock Dodds returned to Bramall Lane for the club's centenary celebrations, and, no doubt, reminisced about derby days of yesteryear. They had their first taste of a League derby in the 1930s, with wing-half Jackson figuring in United's 1-0 win at Hillsborough in October 1933; and Jackson and Dodds played together in the four Second Division derbies between 1937 and 1939 – Dodds scoring in United's 2-1 home win in February 1938.

Len Badger's Testimonial programme 1973.

Joe Shaw on the ball with Bernard Shaw alongside him in a Blades' game in the 1960s.

Premiership Derbies 1992-94

					Wed	Utd
95.	Nov	8	1992	Bramall Lane	1	1
96.	Apr	21	1993	Hillsborough	1	1
97.	Oct	23	1993	Bramall Lane	1	1
98.	Jan	22	1994	Hillsborough	3	1

Len Badger (left) along with Blades colleague Tony Currie and Wednesday skipper Peter Rodrigues after the Badger testimonial match. Also in the picture are United's Geoff Salmons and Tom McAllister.

SHEFFIELD FA CUP DERBIES

Year	Date	Rd	Venue	Wed	Utd
1900	10 Feb	2	Bramall Lane	0	0*
1900	17 Feb	2	Bramall Lane	1	1
1900	19 Feb	2	Owlerton	0	2
1925	31 Jan	2	Bramall Lane	2	3
1928	18 Feb	5	Hillsborough	1	1
1928	22 Feb	5	Bramall Lane	1	4
1954	9 Jan	3	Hillsborough	1	1
1954	13 Jan	3	Bramall Lane	3	1
1960	12 Mar	6	Bramall Lane	2	0
1993	3 Apr	SF	Wembley	2	1†

*Abandoned   †After extra-time

FOOTBALL LEAGUE CUP DERBIES

Year	Date	Rd	Venue	Wed	Utd
1980	9 Aug	1	Hillsborough	2	0
1980	12 Aug	1	Bramall Lane	1	1

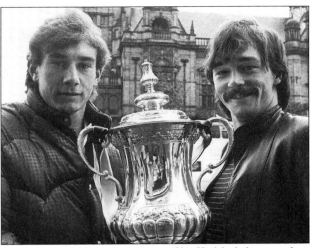

It is over 60 years since a Sheffield club won the FA Cup, but here were two captains who got their hands on the coveted trophy back in 1981 when it was brought to Sheffield for repairs in the city where it was made. Wednesday's Mark Smith (left) and United's Tony Kenworthy savour the moment. and no doubt look forward to the day when a Blade or an Owl can collect it from royal hands at Wembley!

A Football League Cup duel at Hillsborough in 1980. Wednesday's Andy McCulloch battles with United's Martin Peters and John MacPhail.

Derek Dooley, with his grandson Derek, leads out the United and Wednesday teams before his second testimonial match, at Bramall Lane in August 1993

Subscribers

1 Peter D Dabbs
2 Ian P F Dabbs
3 Mr D Thompson
4 P S Pattinson
5 Michael Foster
6 John Davidson
7 Brian David Jeffs
8 Bryan Pell
9 Richard W Taylor
10 David Fletcher
11 M V West
12 S D Rodgers
13 James Bower
14 Adam Bower
15 Richard John Bramall
16 Alan G Holmes
17 Darren Hawksworth
18 David Hawksworth
19 Alan Damms (a Blade)
20 Michael Crapper
21 Michael John Lister
22 Paul Wright
23 Jonathan Edward Lidster
24 Ian N McLean

25 C J Dunk
26 Mr Allan G Podoski
27 Arthur J Hall
28 Mr Roy Spence
29 Robert Stockley
30 R Gill
31 Mark Holland
32 Dennis Graham Ward
33 Micheal John Lee
34 Raymond H Smith
35 Robert Andrew Smith
36 Timmy Greaves
37 David K Harmsworth
38 Alan David Elliott
39 Arthur Eggleston
40 Daniel McLoughlin
41 'Pod'
42 David Brian Everitt
43 Mark R Jones
44 Mr John Slack
45 Mike Paston
46 Nigel J S Ibbotson
47 Colin Ibbotson
48 Stephen, Tammy & Stefan Gambles

49 Thomas Beardshaw

50 Katy Wilkinson (of Worcester)

51 Andrew Richard Clarke

52 Faith & Aussie Walton

53 Mr James Brian Whitham

54 Benjamin M Seth

55 Stephen Franklin

56 Wendy Hollinshead

57 Robert C W Green

58 James Pigott

59 Craig Mitchell

60 Brian T Ward

61 Keith Hall

62 Kevin Wheeldon

63 Mark Sykes

64 Mr J D Knight

65 David Whiteley

66 John Hamre

67 Peter D McLean

68 Ian Brownhill

69 Mr Barry Mettam

70 Stewart Russell Smith

71 A Robertson

72 Cliff Mycock

73 Paul Doughty

74 Garry Eastwood

75 Keith James

76 Ray James

77 Gregory W Lingard

78 Adam Corner

79 Richard Gilson

80 David Whitehead

81 Harry Shillito

82 Brian Speed

83 Claire Roswitha Wilson

84 Paul Tennant

85 D Roy Munn

86 Richard Crooks

87 Alan G North

88 Andrew P Hornsby

89 David J Jeffries

90 John Albert Lyne

91 Mr Peter Fletcher

92 Steven Gary Morris

93 Matthew Anson

94 Martin Green

95 Adrian Scott

96 Christopher John Kidd

97 Jeff Wilson

98 Philip Andrew Grant

99 Elliott Sam Coles

100 Ken & Joan Renwick

101 Philip Harris (Colorado, USA)

102 Steve & Jamie Cryan

103 Paul Haxton

104 David Sloboda

105 Paul M Doherty

106 Andrew Billard

107 David R Malcolmson

108 Ken & Steven Rowles

109 Lee A Bolsover

110 Mark Hubbard

111 Bill Hubbard

112 Adam Kevin Whydle

113 Luke Joseph Whydle

114 Angela Mower (Judson)

115 Patrick Judson

116 Laura Christine Renshaw

117 Steven Mark Westerman

118 Anthony Peal

119 Eric Hilton

120 Winston F Walliss

121 Dean Antony Rhodes

122 Mr F J Perkins

123 John Evans

124 Derek James Fox

125 Mr Edward Spencer

126 Trevor David Bishop

127 Nigel John Cordell

128 Mike Hurley

129 Barrie G Rowan

130 Keith King

131 Dale Vincent Weatherstone

132 Anthony W Rider

133 Nicholas Harrison

134 Roger Green

135 David Mitchell

136 John David Burrows

137 Andrew J & John M Brodie

138 Scott McCabe

139 Simon McCabe

140 Edward Wilby

141 Paul Christopher Darwin

142 David Brodie

143 Robert J Brodie

144 Nathan Mahon

145 C J Woolford

146 G Wilford

147 Simon T Mattock

148 David Middleton

149 David R Kirkland

150 James H Rieuwerts

151 Richard G Hawley

152 Simon J Newsum

153 Anthony W Newsum

154 Mr H Simmonds (NSW, Australia)

155 Walter Glover

156 Ailsa Brookes

157 Alan E Barber

158 Andy Pack

159 Roy Jessop

160 Alan Birchenall

161 Michael Seeds

162 Nigel Pollard

163 Fred Vernon

164 Terry Allen

165 Keith Fowler

166 Brian Owen

167 John Owen

168 F W Hobson

169 Andrew John Hague

170 Pete Watson

171 Michael Grayson

172 Robert Moody

173 Steve Bateman

174 D Rye

175 Jerry Haytack

176 Kevin Wells

177 Elaine & Robert Hargate

178 Helen Knight

179 Mick Woodhead

180 Mr Eric Brammer

181 Ian Bisatt

182 Moira & Terry Woolley

183 Frank Morris

184 Alan David Butler

185 Stephen A Homyard

186 Christopher J Homyard

187 Philip Wilson

188 Dean McCarthy

189 Andrew Douglas Goodman

190 John Jenkinson

191 George Jacklin

192 Mr Ian Brian Nuttall

193 David R Godden

194 Stanley Wraith

195 Stephen Foster

196 M A King

197 Paul Woolfson

198 Nicholas Craig

199 David Bishop

200 William Clarke

201 David Gaimster

202 Frank Beeston

203 Christopher John Jefferies

204 Joe Johnson

205 Gayl R Jackson

206 Rhys Luke Boughen

207 K J Bower

208 Paul Richard Whitaker

209 Lisa Rattenbury

210 Vickie Rattenbury

211 Mr Steven Parkin

212 Adrian Woodward

213 Malcolm Birks

214 Andrew Birks

215 Peter J Currie

216 Keith A Plowman

217 Tony Orwin

218 Leslie John Turner

219 John Albert Lyne

220 Peter L Haigh

221 Michael Thornley

222 David Douglas Bradwell

223 Little Frank Ronksley (Swinton)

224 Christine P Calvert

225 Paul Hague

226 John Paul Garrett

227 Nigel Turner

228 James A Walker

229 Mr Roger P Lee

230 Robert J F Clarkson (Stuff)

231 Richard Pinder

232 Mr G J Parrott (Guernsey)

233 Colin G Soulsby

234 Wayne Bridgeman

235 Lee Vernon

236 Fred Elstone

237 Shaun Antony Beer

238 Matthew James Beer

239 Miss Shelley J Tyson

240 Stephen R Milner

241 John Roy Milner

242 Fraser John Mosley

243 James Murphy

244 A Firth

245 Brian Lewis

246 Adam Paul Clay

247 Anthony John Staniforth

248 Mac Millard

249 M J Foweather

250 Hans Petter Syversen

251 Graham F Watson

252 Mr Andrew Ian Staton

253 Alan Ramsden & Daniel

254 David Vincent Furniss

255 Eleanor O'Shaughnessy

256 Pat & Mavis Ryan

257 Mr Philip Thompson

258 B J Moore

259 James C Cutts

260 David W Helliwell

261 George & Joyce Birtles

262 Michael & Matthew Birtles

263 John Sewell

264 John Wilson

265 Andrew Robinson

266 John McKillop

267 Royce Beal

268 Tom Pearce

269 Leslie Sheard

270 Dawn Harrison

271 Mr F T Smith

272 Ian Hall

273 Barbara Ann Watson

274 Mr Andrew W Moore

275 Jamie King

276 Robert Jackson

277 Peter Law

278 Denis Clarebrough

279 Kevin John Thorpe

280 Paul William Colclough

281 John Cameron Hancock

282 Martin Hoey

283 Raymond Sykes (Ludlow)

284 David R Goddard

285 Christopher J Varley

286 Stuart F Varley

287 Paul S Varley

288 Dean Knowles

289 Arthur R Foreman

290 Mr John Nigel Edmonds

291 Stuart Fish

292 David Goodwin

293 Warren Picker

294 David C Armstrong

295 Robin Howard

296 David Barker

297 Mark Spencer Seagrave

298 David Malcolm Hickin

299 Paul Davis

300 Stephen Robert Naylor

301 Bill E Crowder

302 William L Crowder

303 Michael F Crowder

304 Martin Powell

305 Jordan Mathieson

306 Neil Wilson

307 Gemma Karen Wilson

308 Neil Quail

309 James Oldfield

310 Gary Oldfield

311 Paul Oldfield

312 Simon David Dixon

313 Mark Wheen

314 Mr & Mrs J Nixon

315 Vincent Kenny

316 Norman Johnson

317 Paul Johnson

318 A S Wootton

319 Allison Nixon

320 Stuart Nixon

321 Richard Morton

322 Stephen John Price

323 John Tompkins

324 Russell Ian Davies

235 Steven John Davenport

326 Dean Little

327 Ian D Brooks

328 Niall R Brooks

329 Stuart A Brooks

330 Scotty

331 Mr Stuart Burgin

332 Martin Hawke

333 Richard Grainger

334 Dominic John Stevenson

335 Benjamin Moore

336 Ian Austin Drake

337 Thomas D Price

338 John Mason

339 Andrew Lee

340 Edmund Lee

341 Janet Chrimes (SUFC)

342 Micheal Spowage

343 James Allsopp

344 J M Stannard

345 Harry Jones

346 Alan Palfreyman

347 Stephen James Rennie

348 Martin Mullane

349 Peter O'Carroll

350 Ian Vague

351 George Edward Birch

352 Steven Underhay

353 Arnold Booth

354 Graham K Ward

355 Robert & Andrew Nixson

356 Ryan Wileman

357 Ian Platts

358 R W Burrell

359 Paul Robert Trower

360 David Burkinshaw

361 Alan J Ledger

362 Peter Howarth

363 Emma Jane Howarth

364 F A Siddaway

365 Robert Banner

366 Tom Newcombe

367 Christopher Richard Daykin

368 Robert James Daykin

369 Desmond James

370 Paul Andrew Cross

371 Mark Hallatt

372 Doug Page

373 Steve Haythorne

374 John Ryalls

375 David Webb

376 Barnstoneworth Blades

377 Blades Independent Fans Association

378 Scott Lee Lyons

379 Eric Needham

380 Reg Needham

381 Steven Baines

382 Joanne Buck

383 David Jacques

384 Charles Edward Hodkinson

385 Dale Harrison

386 Simon C Matthews

387 Mr C J Kentzer (SUFC)

388 Mr Richard Fagan

389 Jack Whitehouse

390 Michael J Denial

391 Jordan Mathieson

392 Neil Mathieson

393 Ian Mathieson

394 Stephen Morrill

395 Terry R Allcock

396 Mark Andrew Mather

397 Trevor & Robert Coleman

398 Philip Andrew Ogden

399 Colin Marrison

400 Alan T Ibbotson

401 Paul Robert Lock

402 Christopher Bull

403 Mr Peter Axelby

404 Helen-Claire Stone

405 William Noel Edis

406 Paul M Winter

407 Peter Kay

408 Miss Amanda Wragg

409 Richard Harrison

410 Daniel Roy Regan

411 Terry Regan

412 Thomas James Brammer

413 Z Z Stretch

414 B P Carr

415 Taran Joel Carter

416 Thomas William Gregory

417 Ray Hallam

418 Brian Frith

419 Ian Frith

420 Terry Westwood

421 James Shephard

422 Leonard Thompson

423 James Ian Raikes

424 Michael Blomfield

425 Ernest Callinswood

426 Mr Gerald Heath

427 Gordon Woods

428 Mr Terry Bills

429 Gary Browse

430 Michael S Draper

431 Ernest Barron

432 Steven Kirk